AMERICAN LANGUAGE REPRINTS
SUPPLEMENT SERIES

VOL. 4

A
MISSION DELAWARE
VOCABULARY

By John Ettwein

Edited and Translated by

Raymond Whritenour

Evolution Publishing
Merchantville, NJ
2013

This edition ©2013 Evolution Publishing
Merchantville, New Jersey

Printed in the United States of America

First Edition

Dedicated to Anton, John and Nathaniel,
who taught us how to speak their language.

ISBN 978-1-935228-12-7

Library of Congress Cataloging-in-Publication Data

Ettwein, John, 1721-1802.
A mission Delaware vocabulary / by John Ettwein, edited &
translated by Raymond Whritenour.
    pages cm -- (American language reprints supplement series
; vol. 4)
Includes bibliographical references and index.
ISBN 978-1-935228-12-7 (hardback : alk. paper)
1. Delaware language--Grammar. 2. Delaware language--
Vocabulary. I. Title.
PM1032.E77 2013
497'.3--dc23
                        2013037183

CONTENTS

Introduction

Over a period of about one hundred years, beginning in the mid eighteenth century, seven Moravian missionaries recorded extensive works in the Delaware language. John Ettwein was among the earliest of them. Among his works, Ettwein left us two word lists: one of several pages, included in a 1788 letter now in the papers of George Washington, and, a long manuscript vocabulary of Delaware words and short phrases, with German translation, deposited in the Moravian Archives (Box 333, Folder 1, Item 1) at Bethlehem, Pennsylvania. It is this latter work which is here edited and translated into English..

The manuscript itself is untitled, but the first page has the heading, "J Ettwein." It consists of 44 leaves with 88 unnumbered pages, of which pages 86 and 88 are blank. Page 87 has a single entry—a Biblical half-verse (John1:29b) that serves as a colophon. The word order was intended to follow an alphabetical arrangement; however, many words have been added here and there on most pages, so that the order has become rather haphazard in the final product.

My work on this manuscript consists of establishing the Delaware text, translating the Delaware words and phrases, using Ettwein's German rendering whenever possible and as a guide when it is not, and alphabetizing and indexing the whole. In the vast majority of cases, Ettwein's Delaware text is left as he wrote it, but sometimes his word divisions are wrong and have been corrected here. At times, he chose the "wrong" letter to represent the sound in particular words. Some of these have been corrected in the following text or in a bracketed note. Whenever possible, Ettwein's glosses have been directly translated into English. As mentioned, though, he often recorded no more than a verbal theme, sans subject and/or object, which have been restored in this English translation. Often enough, Ettwein mistook the persons of a verbal phrase. These, too, have been properly rendered into English, here. At all times, the primary goal was to get the Delaware meaning right. Ettwein did not separately enter any but the initial word of a phrase. In this edition, every single Delaware word has been entered in the alphabetical arrangement. The entries which follow each begin with the Delaware word or phrase, followed by an English translation, and ending in a number which indicates on what page of the manuscript that entry can be found. Many of the entries include notes inside brackets, giving information such as how Ettwein spelled the Delaware; how he translated it; what the literal meaning of the entry is; additional data which helps elucidate the meaning of the entry; the initial word of the phrase or phrases in which it can be found; etc. Most of Ettwein's translations are rendered into English in these notes, but others are given in his original German, along with the English—usually when his meaning is not absolutely clear to me—either because he doesn't seem to understand the Delaware, or because I don't understand him; and also, when I think it's needed to support my English translation.

A fair number of readers have come across Zeisberger's dictionary or that of Brinton & Anthony. Ettwein adds a number of lexical gems to this body of work, including words for 'trifolium with the red flowers,' 'the stinging nettle,' 'green clover,' 'a wicker chair,' 'basket wood,' 'rutting deer,' 'buckskin,' 'doeskin,' 'Autumn pelts,' 'Summer pelts,' and a very interesting collection of words for parts of a flintlock rifle, such as 'the rear sight of a gun barrel,' 'a hammer spring,' 'a frizzen spring,' 'a frizzen,' 'a sear,' 'a decorative trim piece,' 'a ramrod holder,' 'a fouling scraper,' and more! A few other unfamiliar Delaware words are recorded, too. (See "woankondis"—a special word used to greet little children.) In all, it seemed a very worthwhile task to bring this vocabulary to public attention.

This manuscript is, demonstrably, a very early work, in which the "standard" Mission Delaware orthography that we see in later works has yet to appear. So, Ettwein's spelling looks rather awkward, at times. For example, he often uses word final "-u" to indicate voiceless "w," after "-k-" (or "-c-"). He also employs "e" and "i," interchangeably, quite a bit, as well as "e" and "a." Besides Jesus, the only real people mentioned are the Indian

Helpers, Anton, John and Nathaniel; and David (probably David Zeisberger, or an Indian of that name). Employment of the term 'little buffalo,' for 'cow,' and the loanword, "teh" ('day'), are other indications that this is a very early work—possibly produced during the 1760's or early 1770's.

With the exceptions noted, pronunciation follows the usual Moravian practice. aa, ee and oo indicate the long vowels (as in father, cliche and note, respectively). Long i (as in machine) is written ie, ij (except after e—see below), or as ii. Long u (as in rule) is written as uu. His breve over a vowel indicates that vowel is short (a as the u in cup, bet, stick, for and hull, respectively). His ü becomes "i" in this edition. Vowels preceding two consonants are generally short, if unmarked. Vowels preceding a single consonant followed by a vowel are generally long. An acute accent indicates primary stress. A circumflex accent indicates aspiration, although it is sometimes difficult to decide whether Ettwein is employing the grave accent for stress or aspiration–just as his macron and breve are hard to distinguish from one another, sometimes. Consonants usually have the same values as in English, with these exceptions: Unvoiced consonants, preceded by a nasal in initial position, or those in final position, preceded by a nasal, are voiced. Thus, mp = mb, nt = nd and nk = ng. The initial nasal is very rarely dropped (in spelling--though it is always there in pronunciation). Since Ettwein used voiced and unvoiced consonants, interchangeably, initial letters which look unvoiced may actually be voiced. Voiced consonants which do not follow nasals are really unvoiced. gu and ku often = kwë. The letter combination, uch usually = voiceless w (though not after sch). So does ch, in final position, when following k. However, ch following an l = voiceless l. Preceding s or t, it usually = h. Everywhere else, ch = ch as in German, Bach, or Scottish, loch. Final position au and eu = a + voiceless w and e + voiceless w, respectively. x is used for both ks and kws. z = ts. ey, eij and ei = i as in English line or sigh. Ettwein's ÿ or ij becomes ij in this edition. The same phonetic value is given to plain y, which is found in word final postition, sometimes. sch is usually written as just sh by Ettwein, but I have used the full sch, which = English sh as in s**h**irt, while tsch = English ch as in lur**ch**. j = y as in English **y**oke.

Grammatical abbreviations are as follows: abv. = absentative; obv. = obviative; sg. = singular; pl. = plural; anim. = animate; inan. = inanimate; ex. = exclusive; incl. or in. = inclusive.

I would like to acknowledge my sincerest thanks to Jim Rementer and Todd M. Thompson for kindly reading this work and offering helpful suggestions and corrections on several entries—and, perhaps, more importantly, for their encouragement of this and other projects, over the years. Entries which bear their contributions are noted inside fancy brackets { }, thus. Jim's read {as per JR} and Todd's read {as per TMT}.

R.W.
Butler, NJ
July 24, 2007

DELAWARE—ENGLISH

-A-

a, could; should; would [see "n'duchwilim"] - 53

a liechsiáne eliechsian, if I knew how to speak the Indian language [lit., 'if I could speak as you (sg.) speak' / Ett: "alligsiáne elligsian"] - 2

A., A. [see "tahicana"] - 73

A. najuumuk, A carried me (on his back) [Ett: 'A carried me across'] - 49

abhittawoapanne, from on high downward [Ett: 'von oben herunter] - 1

abptonewoagan, a word [cp. "aptonacan"] - 1

abtschi k'tahollel, I love you (sg.) always - 1

abtschi lechchauwelemineen, Care for us, always. - 1

abtschi n'dehennanink, always in our hearts - 1

abtschi (n'dellitheham eli) n'mamschala, always will I think of him [lit., 'always (I think of it as) I remember him' - Ett: 'allezeit will ich dran dencken'] - 1

achchumhook, a cloud - 1

achgekútum, a teacher - 1/14

achgeluneuch, he is a liar - 1

achgooktet, a little snake - 1

achgumhokgot, it is cloudy [Ett: 'still, stubborn weather'] - 2

achhuüwoau, it is overcast - 1

achkoolsi, conceal something [see "ki"] - 48

achkoolsoak, they conceal it [Ett: no translation] - 48

achkoolsu, he conceals it - 48

achpijan, you are here [see "gollelendam"] - 15

achpiil, Stay there. [see "na"] - 48

achpiil Kischelemelanggunk, Remain in the Lord. [lit., 'Be there in our Creator'] - 1

achpin, be here [see "tatsch"] - 73

achpitagoch, Abide with you. [see "wulanggunduwoagan"] - 83

achpiwi, is not here [see "atta"] - 5

achpoak, they stay - 51

achpoan, bread [see "atta" & "n'gattotamen"] - 5/60

achquiwi, not to put on [see "atta"] - 5

achwachkummau, it is cloudy - 1

achwatt, it is difficult [Ett. adds '(the life)'] - 1

achwoala, love him [see "n'dallawewe"] - 51

7

achwon, it is strong [see "wusami"] - 84
aacü, Go. (you/pl.) [see "íka"] - 18
ahgoganhillup, he had worms [cp. "w'dachkucumo"] - 4
ahkekentowoagan, a covenant - 1
ahkiwalaau, he is deceived - 2
ahoaltieque, if you (pl.) love each other [Ett: 'if you (pl.) have love'] - 2
aholachtite, if they love him [Ett: 'if he loves you (sg.)'] - 2
ahoollangque, if we (in.) love her [Ett: 'if she loves us'] - 2
ahoollanne, if I love you (sg.) - 2
ahoolitte, if he loves me - 2
âhpitawíneen, Dwell with us. (you/sg.) [see "woak"] — 81
ahtóh, a deer [see "poolguk"] - 68
ahtohoal, a deer (obv.) [see "wünewoawoawall"] - 56
ajanketentammowoagan, indifference - 33
ajaptonaalill, I speak with (you/sg.) [see "gëmauwi"] - 14
aal, Go. (you/sg.) [see "nihiliwi"] - 59
allachimen, rests [see "necama"] - 53
alamink wachtei, inwards; insides [lit., 'within the belly'] - 2
allachchimüin, to rest [Ett: 'Ruhe in' — ?perhaps, a mild command: 'Rest. '] - 2
allachpichsi, talk fast [see "kusámi"] - 36
allamikquaheemi (wikquam), within the house [Ett: "allamik (wikquam) quaheemi"] - 2
allamungque, inward - 2
allappa setpuuk(ch), very early (in the morning) [Ett: 'very early'] - 2
allapawe, early in the morning [see "wulakwet"] - 82
allappi, Listen up! (you/sg.) - 2
allellul, they (obv.) are rotten - 2
allemihillewall, they fly away - 2
allemiú, a corpse - 2
allemussitam, Let us go away. [Ett: "-itammen"] - 2
allemusso, he goes away [see "necama"] - 51
allemusso ju pemmy, he went away until the present [Ett: 'jezt (?)sangt er an'] - 2
allemussoak, they go away - 51
allemussop, Is he gone away? [Ett: "allmussop" & 'Is he already gone away?'] - 2
allennamaane, if I touch it [Ett: 'anrühren durfte'] - 3
allettol, they (inan.) rot [see "metschi"] - 45
allohoacan, a bullet mould - 2

8

allokágan, a servant [E., "allokájan"] - 2
allokuh, he is lean - 2
allowiwe, much better; more [also see "tacu"] - 3/72
allowíwe nolichton, I will improve it - 3
allowiwi, more [see "nostawoake"] - 61
allugákan; allukacan, a messenger; a subject - 3/3
alluhumauwi aneij, Show me the way. (you/sg.) - 3
alluuhumau, Show him. (you/sg.) - 3
allumsijte, if he goes away [Ett: 'Go. Go immediately.' (you/sg.) - 2
allumsouchchwe, Go walk away. (you/sg.) [? "allumouchchwe] [Ett: "-uchche" & 'geh lauf nicht so herum'] - 2
aluut, for - 2
aam, could; should; would [see "atta" & "kattschi" & "kneta" & "ta"] - 5/8/15/20/29/72
amachkoajak, bear-skins - 3
aman, a fish line - 3
amandamwoagan, feeling - 3
amanggieshy, loud (shouts) - 3
amehelleu, it is gone - 3
amemensall, child (obv.); children (obv.) [see "auweeni" & "Jesus"] - 8/18
amemensoak, they are children - 53
amemensoop, he was a child - 53
amemensopannik, they were children - 53
amemensu, he is a child - 53
amenni goossoowall, large wampum belts [?"amanggi" / Ett: 'gr. Belts'] - 3
amimendit, a baby - 3
amimens, a child - 3
amimensemall, children [a possessive form — '(someone's) children'] - 3
amimensoop, he was a child - 25
amimenstook, Children! - 3
amimenstu, little child [lit., 'he is a little child'?] - 11
amimi, a dove [originally, 'a passenger pigeon'] {as per JR} - 3
amimiwak, doves [see previous entry] - 3
amimiwe, a dove [see "natta" & see note on "amimi"] - 49
amoochchol, a canoe [see "gluppigetsch"] - 15
amochchool gochgaheleuch, the canoe is overturned - 3

9

amochchool n'gochgawe, I am under the canoe - 3
amuchk, a beaver - 4
amuchkuwak, beavers - 4
ammuii, Stand up. - 4
ammuijánup, I stood up [Ett: "-jánnup"] - 4
amüíp; amuíp, rose up [see "lapi" & "echogoniechinoop"] - 37/54
amup, he stood up [thus Ettwein - cp. "amüip"] - 4
aamüwe k'tangkamuk, Has a bee stung you (sg.)? - 4
anatschschihineen, Take care of us. (you/sg.) [Ett: 'nun uns gut in acht'] - 4
andahelliil, Conceal me. (you/sg.) - 4
anei; aneij, a way [see "alluhumauwi"] — 3/4
âneke, that [uncertain - see "aween"] - 8
anneschik, I thank you! [Ett: 'thankful, I thank you!'] - 4
anggel, he dies - 4
angeln, be dead; is dead [see "k'tee" & "k'te"] - 24/34
anggellook, they die - 4
anggelloop, he died [also see "Kischellemelang"] - 4/25
angellooppannik, they died - 4
anhauwi, pay [see "kneta"] - 29
anink kpaamsihemmenna, we (in.) are walking in this path - 4
ansipellawon, a plait of hair - 4
Anton wulamallessu, Is Anton well? - 4
apampewiwall n'suppinquool, I weep, gushing forth tears - 4
aptonacan, word [see "machchaaptonágat" - cp. "abptonewoagan"] - 39
apuihilleu(ch), it is easy - 4
apüwaawächtu kehella, cheap enough [lit., 'it is cheap, indeed'] - 4
aschtetehasik m'hittgunk, the Cross - 4
asiskequahoos, a clay pot - 4
aasisku, loam - 4
assuuwi, Sing. (you/sg.) - 4
atta, not [see "necama" & "nik" & "quatsch" & "sok'nink"] - 53/53/56/69/69/71
atta aam n'hitta, it is impossible - 5
atta achtissiwiwak, they are not ripe - 5
atta awulsettammuwi, he is not obedient - 5
atta elinaquatuwi, it does not look so - 5

atta gettemakkelensiwi, you (sg.) are not humble [Ett: 'du bist kein Sunder (herz)'] - 5

atta golhattuwi, Don't you (sg.) have it? - 5

atta haschi, never [Ett: 'nieder'] - 5

atta haschi pennamuwon, I never looked at it [Ett: 'I still haven't looked at it'] - 5

atta hattewi achpoan, I have no bread [lit., 'bread is not here'] - 5

atta heli n'kattatamen, I don't want it - 7

atta hembis achquiwi, I have no shirt [lit., 'there is no shirt to put on'] - 5

atta keku liteháwak, they don't think about it - 5

atta k'lennilúwi, I do not hold you (sg.) - 5

atta k'magenaniwi, Haven't you (sg.) had time? - 5

atta knita, Can't you? - 4

atta kooch achpiwi, Isn't your (sg.) father here? - 5

atta kpendolowi, I don't understand you (sg.) - 6

atta kulituwon, you (sg.) have not made it well - 6

atta lewi, it isn't true - 6

atta maganapiwij, I don't have time - 6

atta mihilussiwi, he is not old - 6

atta milank, we do not give it to him [Ett: "atta milanch" & 'if you (sg.) do not give'] - 6

atta n'delluktawon, I haven't asked you (sg.) [dubious] - 6

atta ndite gemmakehawi, I think I cannot borrow [Ett: 'ich kan nicht borgen'] - 6

atta nemischawi, I have gotten none - 6

atta nenoostammen, I don't understand it - 6

atta n'hitta kecu illuwewij, I cannot speak; I am mute - 6

atta n'hittawi n'damasktiwij, I cannot defecate [Ett: 'ich kan nicht zu stuhl gehen'] - 6

atta nita malennituwon, I cannot make it - 6

atta nita wiite, I cannot go along - 6

atta n'kattammuwij, I don't want it - 7

atta nolamallessiwi, I am not well - 6

atta nolhatuwi, I don't have it - 6

atta nowaháwi, tatsch elkiqü paat, I don't know when he will be coming - 7

atta nowahawiwok, tatsch elkiqü patit, I don't know when they will be coming - 7

atta nowawahowi ta w'telli wulamuen, I don't know if he tells the truth - 7

atta nowawatoowon tatsch, I don't know what I shall do - 7

atta nowawatuwon ta enda gischitung, I don't know where it is made - 7

atta nowewiton, I don't know it - 7

atta n'pendolowi, I don't understand you (sg.) [should be "k'pend-" / Ett: 'I don't understand it' and 'I haven't understood it correctly'] - 6/7

atta ojos golhatuwi, Have you (sg.) no meat? - 6

atta quitachpunggewi, Have you (sg.) no wife? [lit., 'Are you (sg.) not dwelling with someone?' / Ett: 'hastu kein frau'] - 5

atta quitahemeluwe, I don't help you (sg.) [Ett: 'it won't help you (sg.)'] - 7

atta ta lussiwi, I haven't been burnt - 7

atta tendewuíwi, there is no fire [Ett: 'it is no fire there'] - 7

atta thiipigat, it is not a cold night [Ett: 'it will be cold tonight'] - 7

atta wahellemattoowi, it isn't far [Ett: "atta woa-"] - 7

atta wiwunitschawiwij, barren [i.e., 'infertile' (ref. to a female)] - 7

atta wullittuwe, it isn't good - 7

attach k'mechannessiwi, Aren't you (sg.) ashamed of yourself? [? "atta"] - 4

attagoo achpoanawiwi, Isn't there any bread? [Ett: "attagoot" & 'Have you no bread?'] - 6

attagoo kecquiwi, Isn't there any money? [Ett: 'Have you no money?'] - 6

attagoo sisiliesemiwi, Isn't there any cow? [Ett: "attagoot" & 'Have you no cow?' - 'cow' = 'little buffalo'] - 6

athéij, Put out (the fire). (you/sg.) ['aus loschen'] - 7

aatuch; attuch, a deer [see "kechulamähemmo" & "knewauchsa" & "uschummu"] - 21/29/77

atuch uuschummo, a deer horn - 7

aulsettamuwon, you (sg.) are not obedient [see "quatsch"] - 69

auweeke, Use it. (you/sg.) - 8

auween, a person; Who? [also see "wemi"] - 8/8/79

auween na, Who goes there? Who is that? - 8

auween nutikeuch, Who has the watch? [i.e., 'Who's on guard duty?'] - 8

auween pâpohammen, Who knocks (on the door)? - 8

auween wunatamen; aween wunatammen, Who will fetch it? - 8/8

auweeni wunihillalawall amemensall, To whom does the child belong? [lit., 'who owns the child'] - 8

auweniik(ch), who (pl.) [see "wulatenamoak"] - 83

auweentsch hanne nowitschéwo, Who will I go with? [Ett: 'Who goes with you?'] - 8

auwimaalen, whoring - 8

auwohuch, he is known [see "seeki"] - 71

auwottawone aam, if I know it rightly - 8

aawechelan, a fine rain - 9

awechimoosak, animals - 8

aawehellewak, they fly away [see "N."] - 9

awejajissook, they are animals [Ett: "awejagissook"] - 8

aween, Who? [cp. "auween"] - 8

aween katta âneke, Who wants that? - 8

aween k'tellsettawan, From whom have you (sg.) heard that? - 8

aween nan, Who is that? - 8

aween pijsqutu, Who farted? [Ett: 'Who has been acting impurely?'] - 9

aween uchtaan, Who has gone there? [Ett: "… nuchtaan"] - 8

aween wunatammen [see "auween wunatamen"]

aweeni pmihilla, What (anim.) flies there? - 8

awich, Astonishing! - 9

awihilew elichsijek(ch), your (pl.) speech is funny - 9

awimalachummook, dogs in heat - 9

awimalatook, rutting deer - 9

awischachkallukassa, he always torments him (with mockery) - 9

awossagame, heaven - 9

awossijajittite, if they are on the other side [Ett: 'Warme dich an der ander seide' ('Warm yourself on the other side.')] - 9

awossy, Warm yourself. (you/sg.) - 9

awulsettammuwi, not obedient [see "atta"] - 5

-B-

bakhakku, a board [cp. "packchäk" & "pachhak"] - 9
balleton, spoil it - 9
bambil, a book [see "tschitannen"] - 76
bengwiquammen, to dry it off (with a towel) {as per TMT} [Ett: "benwiqu-" & no translation] - 9
bescheweuwak, they brought (someone) - 9
Bethlehem, Bethlehem [see "elitsch" & "kigischquike"] — 12/23
Bethlehem guttasch teh ummenneep, he came from Bethlehem six days ago [Ett: 'I came from ...'] - 9
Bethlehem n'dahn, I go to Bethlehem - 9
Bethlehem ummen, he comes from Bethlehem [Ett: 'I come from ...'] - 9
bingschiwanak, eyeballs - 10
bîson, medicine - 10
bolkun, he swims away [lit., 'he flees'] - 10
bolluk, he's off [lit., 'he flees'] - 10
bugqühelleu, broken - 10
bugquihellewatsch, he will break - 10
bunito, Let it be. (you/sg.) [also see "sche"] - 9/70

-C-

chánsa, elder brother (abv.) [see "ki"] - 23
choeij, a pelt [see "k'matschalla"] - 28
chucque, Cough once. (you/sg.) - 10
chunn, snow - 10
clammiche, Hold still. - 10

-D-

dachchineen, Stay by us. (you/sg.) - 10
dachpehellatsch, it will echo; it will sound - 10
dachquihelleu, it goes to seed - 10
dachachson, lead (the metal) - 10
daholuk, he loves me [Ett: 'he loves you'] - 10
dangkamukky, let blood - 10
dappuschuwak, they roast - 10

David, David [see "ehohlak"] - 11

dee, heart - 10

dellagammal n'tallikki, you (sg.) must lend me [dubious] - 11

delangomaneen, our friend [lit., 'we (ex.) are friendly with him'] - 10

demahican, a hatchet with handle; an ax [also see "haanhug-wiitu" - cp. "tmahican"] - 10/17

depalingquehellage, it is ripe enough - 11

doctel quikehawall, the doctor has healed him - 11

duchwilu Nathaniel, Nathaniel is a good hunter — 11

-E-

eccomi, song; hymn - 11

ehachpusitung, a gridiron - 11

ehachtubuwing, a cup - 11

ehamhitehûkuk, the battery on a gunlock; frizzen [also see "manihtu" — part of the gunlock mechanism] - 11/42

ehellekikehond mikon, a pen [i.e., 'a writing quill'] - 11

ehohlak nimat David, dear brother David [lit., 'him whom I love, my brother, David'] - 11

ehoolak, him whom I love [Ett: 'my lover'] - 11

eholanquiik, those whom we love [Ett: 'our lover'] - 11

ehoolaat, she who loves him [Ett: 'his lover'] - 11

eholaatitschi, him whom they love [Ett: 'their lover'] - 11

eholaatschi, her whom he loves [Ett: 'his lover'] - 11

eholaatschiik, him whom they love [Ett: 'their lover'] - 11

eholekquik, those whom you (pl.) love [Ett: 'your lover'] - 11

eholon, my lover; one whom I love [thus Ettwein on 11 - also see "ni"] - 11/58

ehoowoalak, him whom I love [Ett: 'your (sg.) lover'] - 11

ehowoalan, him whom you (sg.) love [Ett: 'lover'] - 11

ehowoalatschik, him whom they love [Ett: 'their lover'] - 11

ehowoaleek, him whom you (pl.) love [Ett: 'your (pl.) lover'] - 11

ehowoalekque (amimenstu), when you (pl.) love him (the little child) [Ett: 'to love (children)'] - 11

ehoowoalenk, him whom we (ex.) love [Ett: 'our lover'] - 11

ehundakbank, where one repeatedly shuts things in [i.e., "ehenda kpahank" - very uncertain - Ett: no translation] - 11

éjabtschi, still [see "nen"] - 56

ékk'hokgeewiit, people; nation [see "weemi"] - 79

ekitsch nipung, Summer will begin [Ett: 'Sommers anfang'] - 11

ekkulij, swift - 11

el, Say it. (you/sg.) [see "N." - cp. "eelch"] - 43

elagkuschik, a staircase - 11

elaloge, what is worked [see "machtetsu"] - 40

elalogunk, that which is worked [see "mechheek"] - 43

elanggomachquik, those to whom I'm related [Ett: 'm. f.' - i.e., 'my friends'] - 52

élank, as we (incl.) say to him [see "kimachtenna"] - 25

elaptonnétup, how he spoke [Ett: 'what was said'] - 11

elauchsiit, he who lives so [Ett: 'he who lives'] - 11

elawachtiik, ransom - 11

eelch, Tell it. (you/sg.) [cp. "el"] - 52

elemegisquik, today - 12

elemegisquik lapi n'pah, I come again today - 12

elemoqunaga, afterwards - 12

eelgigunk, as wide as [see "schi"] - 87

eli, as; because [see "abtschi" & "gollelendam" & "pitschtá" - cp. "heli"] - 1/15/67

eli newoap, as I saw him [Ett: "elinewoap" and 'I have seen'] - 12

eli peekok hokkey, as his body is wounded [i.e., '... has holes' - Ett: 'on your wounded body'] - 12

eli pendilehillak, a pilot hole [i.e., for a muzzle-loading gun] [Ett: 'ein Zundloch'] - 12

eli tekkennowiik, in the woods [Ett: 'I was in the bush'] - 12

eli weelaquik, this evening [lit., 'while it is evening'] - 12

eli wulaquike, last night [lit., 'while it is night'] - 12

elichsijek, the way you (pl.) speak [see "awihilew"] - 9

elichsilitschi, languages - 12

elícus, an ant - 12

elicusak, ants - 12

eliechsian, how you (sg.) speak [see "a" & "n'gatta"] - 57

elijan, for that - 15

elikigamek; elikigomek, an ant-hill - 12/12

elilawejachsit, faces - 12

elilawejakusit, faces - 12

16

elimihillat, one who flies away - 12
elinaquatuwi, not look so [see "atta"] - 5
elithehattamáchtître, as they think about it [Ett: no translation] - 12
elithehattamaane, as I think about it [Ett: no translation] - 12
elithehatameque, as you (pl.) think about it [Ett: no translation] - 12
elithehattank, he who thinks about it [Ett: "-hattan" & no translation] - 12
elitsch gisquik jüh nachóak nimattak pewak Bethlehem, today three of my brethren will come to Bethlehem [Ett: "... pawak ..."] - 12
elkhiqui tpisgawihillak, at the appointed time - 13
elkikung hakkij, the World; Earth [lit., 'as wide as the Earth'] - 2
elkiqui, like-as [see "atta"] - 7/7
clowéza, hc has said [see "Jesus"] - 18
elowiyan, what you (sg.) say [see "kehella"] - 22
eelsiechtit, as they do [see "necamawa"] - 12
eelsija, as I do [see "ni"] - 12
elsijan, as you (sg.) do [see "ki"] - 12
eelsijank, what we (incl.) do [see "kiluna"] - 24
eelsijeek, as you (pl.) do [see "kiluwa"] - 12
eelsijenk, as we (ex.) do [see "niluna"] — 12
eelsijenk n'dêhennanink, as we (ex.) are in our (ex.) hearts [Ett: "eelsijank" and 'it is in our hearts'] - 12
eelsit, as he does [see "necama"] - 12
emhoonis, a spoon [Ett: no translation] - 40
enda, where [see "atta"] - 7
endeneep, were so; was so [see "küwingi" & "ni"] - 36/60
enenthakewoacan; enenthakkewoagan, parable; simile - 12/13
epiángque, where we (incl.) are - 19
epiank, where we (incl.) are [see "ukke"] - 77
eschoochwê, You (sg.) must go through. [Ett: "-oochê] - 13
esco, not yet - 13
esco sokenuppassiquik/ch/, the unbaptized [lit., 'they who are not yet baptized'] - 13
esquaata, not yet - 13
esquo teppelentamowi, he does not yet have enough [Ett: 'not yet enough' - one might expect "... teppelentamowun"] - 13

esquo wingoiwi, it is not yet ripe [Ett: 'not yet ripe'] - 13

eet, perhaps [see "kehella" & "kigischquike" & "n'duchwilim" & "quatsch" & "ta" & "wahelemat"] - 22/53/69/ 73/73/78

etspinaquat, color - 13

-F-

Frh., Frh. [uncertain, probably 'Friedenshuetten,' see "nowi-ki"] — 61

-G-

gaachannekeetsch, See whether it will begin. [Ett: "-anne keetsch" & 'Sieh ob es angeht'] - 13

gachgihella, break it down - 13

gachgihilleuchtsch, it will break [Ett: "-hilleluch"] - 13

gachkenne, break it down - 13

gachpétoon, to loosen - 13

gachtingeuchtsch, next year - 14

gakkelemíme, Think of me (you/sg.). [fut. imp.] - 13

gaakun k'tschihilleuch, the stocking hangs down - 13

gamink k'dahemenook, Do we (incl.) go across? [Ett: 'Do you go across?'] - 13

gamink n'dahemmenna, we (ex.) go across - 13

gaamunk, on the other side [see "gëmennach"] - 14

gatta pennawo, Do you (sg.) want to see him? [Ett: "gatta penna wo" & 'Do you desire to see it?' - "-awo" = "-awa"] - 13

gattatam, you (sg.) desire something; you (sg.) want something - 13/57

gattatammen, you (sg.) desire it - 13

gattatammenéwo, you (pl.) desire it - 13

gattatamohenna, we desire it - 1

gattemakejanku, we (incl.) inherited - 14

gathamáwa, to inherit - 14

gauwi, you (sg.) sleep - 58

gauwihimmo, you (pl.) sleep - 58

gauwihummenaagup, we slept - 58

gauwihummogup, you (pl.) slept - 58

gauwihump, you (sg.) slept - 58

gauwin, he sleeps; it (anim.) sleeps - 14/58

gauwitool, I sleep with you (sg.) [see "gëmauwi"] - 14

gauwiwak, they sleep - 58

gechhena weelmukquenk, Our Protector [likely a name for God] - 14

gechkauwink, a bed [see "ni"] - 58

gechkauwit, his bed [see "necama"] - 53

gegummenna, our money - 58

gegummennanall, our monies [see note on "n'geegumall"] - 58

gegummuwoa, your (pl.) money - 58

gegummuwoawoll, your (pl.) monies [see note on "n'geegumall"] - 58

gehetéki, a few straps [see "kepahonung"] - 23

gekegutemekque, a teacher - 14

gemmakehawi, I cannot borrow [see "atta"] - 6

gëmauwi ajaptonaalill, I come to speak with you (sg.) [Ett: 'I am come to speak'] - 14

gëmauwi gauwitool, I come to sleep with you (sg.) [Ett: 'I am come to sleep'] - 14

gëmauwi glistool, I come to listen to you (sg.) [Ett: 'I am come to hear] - 14

gëmauwi migentamool, I come to work for you (sg.) [Ett: 'I am come to work'] - 14

gëmauwi wipómel, I come to eat with you (sg.) {as per JR} [Ett: 'I am come to eat'] - 14

gëmauwi witschisemoomell, I come to drink with you (sg.) [Ett: 'I am come to drink'] - 14

gëmennachk gaamunk, over your (sg.) fence [Ett: "-mennach gaa-"] - 14

gëmilaan, you (sg.) give it to him - 14

gëmilaneen, we (incl.) give it to him - 14

gëmilanewo, you (pl.) give it to him - 14

gëmilawoowok, you (pl.) give it to them - 14

gëmilen, I give it to you (sg.) - 14

gëmiilenneen, we give it to you - 14

gëmilennewo, I give it to you (pl.) - 14

gëmilguun, he gives it to you (sg.) - 14

gëmilgunaanak, they give it to us (in.) - 14

gëmiliin, you (sg.) give it to me - 14

gëmilíneen, you give it to us - 14

genameluhemmenna, we thank you - 14
gennenoostawatimmenna, we (incl.) understand each other [see "kiluna"] - 24
gentaquahellen, to nail on - 14
geschiechtoon, you (sg.) wash it - 57
geschiechtonewa, you (pl.) wash it - 57
Getannetowiit, He Who is the Great Spirit [see "schi" - cp. "Kettannittuwid"] - 87
gettemakkelensijenk(ch), we (ex.) are humble [Ett: 'we are not poor'] - 14
gettemakkelensiwi, you (sg.) are not humble [Ett: adds, in parentheses, "(heart)" - see "atta"] - 5
gettemakhattenamoagan, poverty - 14
g'hella, indeed [same as "kehella" - see "kella"] - 22/22
giigeehelachk [see "kigeéhellachk"]
gischachgeenintowoagan, judgment [Ett. "-imtowoagan"] - 14
gischachsommawíneen, Enlighten us. (you/sg.) - 14
gischcu, day [see "taccan"] - 72
Gischellemijan, My Creator! - 14
gischgihilleuch, it is cut in two [Ett: 'cut in two']- 14
gischitung, it is made [see "atta"] - 7
gischquik, it is day; today [see "jukke" & "machchaaptoná- gat" - cp., "gisquik"] - 19/39
gischuuchochki, month; months [see "gutte" & "nischa"] - 16/16
giskaquen, to chop wood - 14
gisquik, it is day [see "elitsch" - cp., "gischquik"] - 12
gispe, I am sated [see "teepi"] - 74
gitelentsch, thumb - 14
glamhattenamoácan, steadiness - 15
gliestamenke, if we (ex.) listen; if we (ex.) hear [Ett: "-meke"] - 14
glistool, I listen to you [see "gëmauwi"] - 14
gluppiangque, if we (incl.) turn around - 15
gluppigetsch amoochchol, Let the canoe turn around [Ett: 'Turn the canoe around.'] - 15
gluppihum aam ki, you should turn yourself around [Ett: 'you have turned yourself'] - 15
gooch, your (sg.) father - 60
goochenook, our father - 60
gochgahelleuch, it is overturned - 3

gogochpopetechen, it is the pulse - 14

goohum, your (sg.) grandmother [see "witschem"] - 81

goingaappin, Are you (sg.) willing to be here? [Ett: 'Will you stay here?'] - 15

golangguumgunatsch Kischellemelang, the Savior will bless us (in.) [lit., 'our Creator will be friendly to us] - 15

goolche(ch); golche(uch), it smokes - 15/68

gollelendam eli achpijan, Are you (sg.) glad because you (sg.) are here? [Ett: 'Fr.l. freust du dich das du in fah. wohnst'] - 15

gollelendamen, you (sg.) are glad [Ett: "gollendmen"] - 15

gollemikitolen ksitink, I worship you at your feet [Ett: "-enk sitink" and only 'at your (sg.) feet'] - 15

goolháttu; golhattu, Have you (sg.) ...? (e.g., 'meat' or 'bread,' etc.) [also see "kpachkschican"] - 15/31

golhattuwi; golhatuwi, Don't you (sg.) have it? [see "atta"] - 5/6

golike, for that - 15

gollséttam, you (sg.) believe [see "jukke"] - 19

golsettammen, you (sg.) believe it - 61

goolsettamoehalguua, he makes you (pl.) faithful [Ett: 'make us faithful'] - 15

goschiechtoon, he washes it - 57

goschiechtonewa, they wash it - 57

goschimui, you (sg.) run away - 68

goossoowall, wampum belts [see "amenni"] - 3

gottatammenéwo, they desire it - 13

gowijosum, your (sg.) meat - 65

guchoowáh, your (pl.) father - 60

guuchwëüch, from behind - 15

gulasúwij N., You (sg.) sing well, N.. - 16

gulatenami, Are you (sg.) amused? - 16

gunaksu m'hittuk, it (anim.) is a tall tree [Ett: "gunaku"] - 16

gunalachkat, it is a deep hole - 15

gunapegkichsu, he speaks slowly - 16

gunaquat, it is tall - 16

gundácan, throat; my gullet - 16

gunten, you (sg.) get it from [conjectural - see "ta"] - 73

gusamósommo, you have drunk too much - 16

guschschachsi, Are you (sg.) in the smoke? - 16

guttasch, six [see "Bethlehem"] - 9
gutte, one - 16
gutte gischuuchochki, one month - 16
gutte kischku, one day - 16
gutte spiegkeiju, one limb - 16
guttelliku, after his kind - 16
gutten, once [see "tschitsch"] - 76
guttkúwak, your (sg.) knees - 16
guttschilachtool, Try it. (you/sg.) - 16
guttschliwindasu, named - 16
guttúchen, it is only one -16

-H-

hä; ha, it is asked [question particle - see "taa"] - 73/73/73
habwoagan, a tobacco pipe - 10
hackey, the body - 17
hakkeng hattu, Lay it on the ground - 17
hakki; hakkij, the Earth; ground [see "elkikung" & "na" & "schi"] - 2/48/87
hakkij kachteu, the earth (the ground) is dry - 17
hakking, low - 17
hakko, on the ground [dubious - see "Kischellemelang"] - 26
hakquai, croup - 17
hallachpisak, Indian hemp - 17
hallamacamik, eternal - 17
hallapangel, a barrel - 17
hallemiwoaniu, it vanished - 17
hamanak, a rod and line with which to fish - 17
hanne, it is asked [question particle - see "auweentsch"] - 8
haanhugwiitu demahican, Encase the ax for me. (you/sg.) - 17
haschi, ever [see "atta"] — 5/5
haskeewak, fresh (meat) - 17
hassis, a horse [see "peschume"] - 66
hassissischqunneij, horse-hair [lit., 'a horse's tail'] - 17
hattape, a bow - 17
hattéu, it is there [see "ika"] - 18
hattewi, it is not here [see "atta"] - 5
hattu, Lay it. (you/sg.) [see "hakkeng"] - 17
heekee lewonneen, Oh, no! Is it possible? [Ett: 'Is it possible?'] - 17

heli, as [see "atta" - cp. "eli"] - 7
hembis, a shirt [see "atta"] - 5
hentachquahasik, a hand-mill - 17
higachquan, shin-bone - 17
hilachten, a mountain gorge [Ett: 'Rinne vom Berg'] - 17
hokappehellat, a decorative trim piece [i.e., for a rifle] [see
    "mallenítu"] - 42
hokkenam, his body [one might expect "hokkejum"] - 17
hokkey, his body [see "eli"] - 12
hoktschaktschessi, a frizzen spring [part of the gunlock
    mechanism] - 17
hokkung n'dahn, I go up - 17
hoos, a kettle [see "tangeto" — cp, "huus"] - 73
hoosch, a kettle [see "kschehélal"] - 32
huiktschi, a breech screw [see "mallenítu"] - 42
hupuchquenenam, side of the body - 17
huus, a kettle [Ett: no translation at 40 - cp. "hoos"] - 17/40
husca, very [Ett: "huska" - also see "n'schaússi"] - 18/62
husca noliwunéwo, I do not see him very well [an odd form
       - one would expect "atta husca noli newoawi"]
    - 18
husca théu, it is very cold - 18
husca wullessu m'hittuck, it (anim.) is a very beautiful tree
    - 18
husca wullit, it is very good [Ett: 'very, very good'] - 18
huscatek nolapematsch, I will use it very well - 18

-I-

ijoon, this (inan.) [see "machchaaptonágat" - cp. "jun"] - 39
ika, there [see "nihiliwi" - cp. "ukke"] - 59
íka aacü, Go there. (you/pl.) [Ett: "Go."] - 18
ika hattéu; ika hatteü, it is there [Ett: 'I have it' - also see
    "ojoos"] - 18/65
illuwewij, he does not speak [see "atta"] - 6
isquandei, a door [see "kpahij"] - 31
itspiê Lenappe, a foreign Indian [Ett: "itspiêl ... - prob.
    "tschipi"] - 18

-J-

Jesu, Jesus [see "wulatenamoak"] - 83

Jesum, my Jesus [see "newótsch"] - 56

Jesus, Jesus [see "ni"] - 60/60

Jesus elowéza, Jesus has said [Ett: 'Jesus has once said'] - 18

Jesus k'taholgunok, Jesus loves us (in.) - 18

Jesus weemi amemensall w'taholawall, Jesus loves all children - 18

jetta nelak, gone nowhere - 18

Joh., John [see "ktellauchsa"] - 35

joheka, forefinger [cp. "luhikan"] - 18

ju, here [see "allemusso" & "na" & "tatsch" & "wahelemat"] - 2/48/48/48/73/78

ju lenni, Make it so. (you/sg.) [or, 'Hand it here.' (you/sg.) - Ett: "jul lenni"] - 19

ju shakkij, so long; so far - 19

juch tendeuche, Make a fire. (you/sg.) [Ett: "tendeuchwe"] - 19

juch witschemil, Help me. (you/sg.) - 19

juch wiitschéwijl, Go with me. (you/sg.) - 19

juchta mattschitam, Come, let us go. [Ett: "jûh k'ta mattschitamen" - lit., 'Now, let us go home.'] - 18

juchta schunnijk, You (pl.) must barter. - 19

jüh, well [emphatic - see "elitsch"] - 12

jûh leemattappê pecho m'pa, Well, sit down. (you/sg.) I will come soon. - 18

jûh nachkohomauwi, Sing me a verse. (you/sg.) [i.e., 'Do sing.'] - 18

jukke, now [see "lawoapanne" & "machchaaptonágat" & "na"] - 37/39/48

jukke gollséttam, now you (sg.) believe - 19

jukke k'majawina, now you (sg.) straighten him out [Ett: 'jezt hast du recht'] - 19

jukke mootsch gischquik, today is Atonement Day [thus Ettwein] - 19

jukke némen, now I see it - 19

jukke weemi epiángque, now we (incl.) are all here - 19

jukkela k'timinaquoan, Good luck to you (sg.) [lit., 'Oh that you (sg.) will be lucky!'] - 19

jukkela ni, I wish [lit., 'Oh that I'] - 19

jul, these (inan.) [see "kattatammen" & "ki"] - 20/24

julak, on this side - 19
julak gumenneen, we come from there - 19
jun, this (inan.) [see "knennámen" & "mili" & "n'dakkindamen"
    - cp. "ijoon"] - 29/47/51

-K-

k', you [prefix] - 56
kachbeton, to be bound [i.e., 'tied'] - 19
kachgélen, to keep - 19
kachkihilla, you (sg.) are broken. - 19
kachkihillewatsch, it will be broken — 19 [usual spelling:
    "kachkihilleuchtsch"]
kachpateung, east wind - 4
kachpéhsa, a twin (abv.) - 19
kachpéhsak, twins - 19
kachteu, it is dry [see "hakkij"] - 17
kachtiname, years old [see "keche"] - 21
kachtuepi, your (sg.) body [Ett: "sach-"] - 48
kähawees, your (sg.) mother [see "ta" - cp. "khahoes"] - 73
kakeluwanne, you (sg.) are a liar [thus Ettwein] - 20
kakkiwallij, you (sg.) deceived me - 20
kakkiwallukke; kakkiwalúke, Are you (sg.) deceived? [Ett: 'I
    am deceived' for the first form] - 20/20
kandschoctican, a flashpan [see "maníhtu"] - 42
kanschuweu, it bangs [or 'reports,' 'cracks,' etc.] - 20
käschikan, a sponge [probably pronounced, käs'chikan] - 20
katta, want [see "aween"] - 8
katta luhumulen, I want to teach you (sg.) - 20
katta mahallamen, Do you (sg.) want to buy it? - 20
katta sognupasewe, Don't you (sg.) want to be baptized? [Ett:
    'Won't you get baptized?'] - 5
kattatammen jul, Do you (sg.) desire this? [lit., Do you desire
    these?] - 20
katschi aam, You must not say so. [idiomatic or lacking a
    word?] - 20
kattschi k'mischschamsa, Oh! You (sg.) have gotten it. [Ett:
    'o hast du ? gekriegst] - 20
kattschi k'paamse, O, you (sg.)! Have you already gotten
    here? [thus Ettwein] - 20
kattschi makamene, Wait! Wait! [thus Ettwein]- 20

kattschi miliégetsch, Oh! Give him nothing. (you/sg.) [thus
    Ettwein — lit., 'Don't let him be given it.'] - 20
kattschi pababi, Don't play. - 20
kattschi pallestamowi tschuk wullesta, Do not disbelieve,
    but believe. (you/sg.) [Ett: 'Sez nicht unglaubig,
    sondern glaubig'] - 20
katschi ponihan, Don't let me go. (you/sg.) - 21
kaatschi sooka, Don't pour it out. (you/sg.) - 21
katschi wannessi, Don't forget it. (you/sg.) - 21
kauwiill, Go to sleep. (you/sg.) - 21
kauwin, you (sg.) sleep - 73
k'bambilum, your (sg.) book [see "ta"] - 73
k'dahemenook, we (in.) go [see "gamink"] - 13
k'dahoolgunook, he loves us (in.) [i.e., 'all of us'] - 33
k'dahoolguwoa, he loves you (pl.) - 33
k'daholuk, he loves you (sg.) - 33
k'dakgolsihummo, you (pl.) conceal it - 48
k'damemensi, you (sg.) are a child - 53
k'damemensihimmo, you (pl.) are children - 53
k'damemensihimmogup, you (pl.) were children - 53
k'damemensihump, you (sg.) were a child — 53
k'damiku, you enter [conjectural — see "quatsch"] - 69
k'daan, your (sg.) daughter - 10
k'daanak, your (sg.) daughters - 10
k'daanuwoawak, your (pl.) daughters - 10
k'daanuwôh, your (pl.) daughter - 10
k'dappi, you (sg.) stay - 51
k'dappihimmo, you (pl.) stay -51
k'dappihump, you (sg.) stayed - 51
k'dappinewoagup, you (pl.) stayed - 51
k'de [see "k'te"]
k'dellaaneep, you (sg.) told him - 52
k'dellaanewoagup, you (pl.) told him - 52
k'delangooma, your (sg.) friend - 52
k'delatquehi, you (sg.) lent me [Ett: 'I am indebted to you']
        - 21
k'dellatquehuke, you (sg.) are indebted - 21
k'delatquéhul, I lent you (sg.) [Ett: 'you are indebted to me']
        - 21
k'dellenemen, you (sg.) make it [see "kecu"] - 30
k'dellitehamsa, Have you (sg.) thought about it? - 21
kduulhäl, your (sg.) breast [i.e., 'chest'] - 21

26

keaachoak, How many? (of living creatures) - 21

kechangquechtu, How many fathoms? - 21

keche kachtiname, How old are you? - 21

keche muschammu, How many fathoms? - 21

keche wunannitu, How many fathoms? - 21

kecheti mili, Give me a little of it. (you/sg.) - 21

kechiti, a little [see "petanne"] - 66

kechulamähemmo aatuch, How many deer have you (pl.) killed? [Ett: 'How many deer has he?'] - 21

kecquiwi, there is not anything [see "atta"] - 6

kecu; keku, What?; How?; a thing; what; something [also see "atta" & "kemauwi" & "mili" & "tacu" & "wemi" & "woak"] - 5/6/28/30/47/72/79/81

kecu elowunssu, What is his name? - 30

kecu k'dellenemen, What do you (sg.) make? - 30

kecu ketátamen, What do you (sg.) desire? [Ett: 'What will you have?'] - 30

kecu kmilani, What will you (sg.) give me? [thus Ettwein - one might expect "kmili"] - 30

kecu ktellichton, What will you (sg.) make? - 30

kecu lallogeuch, What has he made? - 30

kecu leuch kpayachkhikan, How is your (sg.) gun? [Ett: "kpayachhikan" & 'What will you have done to your gun?'] - 30

kecu lowonsu, What is he named? - 30

kecu manittuwak, What do they make? - 30

kecu mekindamen, What do you (sg.) work? - 31

kecu mitschijeksa, What have you (pl.) eaten? - 31

kecu najuntam, What does he carry? - 49

kecu najuntammen, What do I carry? [Ett: 'What do you carry?'] - 49

kecu pendamenke, if we (ex.) hear something [Ett: 'What do you (sg.) hear?'] - 31

kecu wdeloendamen, What is that called? [lit., 'What does he call it?' - Ett: "deloen-"] - 30

kecu welitamen, What did you (sg.) make? - 31

kecüak; kecuak, wampum beads [see "n'sukkéhaak" & "wewoapsitschik"] - 62/79

kegüm, your (sg.) money - 58

kegümall, your (sg.) monies [see note on "n'geegumall"] - 58

kehakkegiimguneen, we (incl.) are becoming learned [lit., 'he teaches us (incl.)'] - 23

27

këhella; **kehella,** indeed [see "apüwaawächtu" & "Kischellemelang" & "kitschiwi" & "na" - cp. "g'hella"] - 4/25/27/48

kehella eet, it is so [lit., 'indeed, perhaps'] - 22

kehella kitschiwi, it is truly so [lit., 'indeed, truly'] - 22

kehella nanne leuch elowijan, Is what you (sg.) say the truth, indeed? - 22

kehella n'gattuupwe, I am surely hungry [Ett: "... -uupe"] - 22

kehella nowingi lissinen, indeed, we (ex.) will do it willingly [Ett: 'I will do it willingly'] - 22

kehella schachachki leu, indeed, it is the pure truth - 22

kekok, wampum beads [Ett: no translation] - 40/65

keku [see "kecu"]

kella g'hella kulichsin, Oh yes, you speak well - 22

kella g'hella pommauchsu, yes, he yet lives - 22

keliuhoggaleltsch, I will comfort you (sg.) [Ett: "-letsch"] - 61

keloolhtoweuch, she quarrels - 27

kemauwi kecu lij, Do you (sg.) come to say something? [i.e. 'Do you (sg.) come to tell me something?'] - 28

kemauwi lukuun, he comes to tell you (sg.) [Ett: "ruf wie N."] - 28

kemauwi newull, I come to see you (sg.) - 22

kemilen, I give it to you (sg.) [Ett: 'will dir de schenken'] - 22

kemootkeu, he steals [Ett: 'you have stolen'] - 22

kenámuck, he thanks you (sg.) - 22

kenduwenn, week [see "taccan"] - 72

kensch lenny, instantaneously - 22

kensch ummennewoacup, that instant, they came from (somewhere) [Ett: 'that instant, they are gone away'] - 22

kepahonung gehetéki, a few straps on the door [Ett: 'ein paar Bänder' - no translation of the first word] - 23

kepe, you (sg.) too [Ett: "koepoek"] - 21

kepe kschisu k'te, Is your (sg.) heart also pure? [Ett: "koepoe ..."] - 21

kepe quitschewulen, Shall I go along with you (sg.) too? [Ett: "koepoek ..."] - 21

kequoll, wampum beads (obv.) [Ett: no translation] - 65

keschingquemsaa woak k'schilemsk'schemsa, Have you (sg.) washed your face and hands? - 23

Kettannittuwid, the Almighty [lit., 'He Who is the Great Spirit' - cp. "Getannetowiit"] - 23

ketatamen, you (sg.) desire it [see "kecu"] - 30

ketelliteha, Do you (sg.) think so? - 23

kgischenakusiwi, you (sg.) are not ready [see "nescota"] - 56

khahoes, your (sg.) mother [cp. "kähawess"] - 60

khahoesall, his mother - 60

khahoésennook, our (incl.) mother - 60

khahoesoowâh, your (pl.) mother - 60

khahoesowoawall, their mother - 60

khigachquan, your (sg.) shin-bone - 23

k'higauwihuk, he lends you (sg.) [see "na"] - 48

khíke, you (sg.) mend in health [see "metschi"] - 44

khikëunge, they (abv.) mend in health [see "metschi"] - 44

k'hikkewonn, your (sg.) nose - 23

khikkínammenneen, we recognize it [see "n'dallemi"] - 51

k'hukqui, your (sg.) chin - 23

ki, you (sg.) [also see "gluppihum" & "n'tahoalel"] - 15/56/ 60

ki achkoolsi, you (sg.) conceal it [Ett: no translation] - 48

ki chánsa, your (sg.) elder brother (abv.) - 23

ki elsijan, as you (sg.) do [Ett: no translation] - 12

ki jul k'tallitoon, Did you (sg.) make these? - 24

ki ktayábtoon, you (sg.) talk, 24

ki k'tê kischuésu, Is your (sg.) heart warm? - 24

ki kwiwall, your (sg.) wife - 24

ki metsche tendeücheen, Did you (sg.) make a fire, already [Ett: Have you made fire?'] - 25

ki mohoccu, your (sg.) blood - 25

ki neetammi wisachkamallessijanneep, you (sg.) first felt bitter pain [Ett: 'your painful first birth'] - 25

ki quitschewi, you (sg.) go with me - 62

ki suugenupássi, Are you (sg.) baptized? - 27

ki wechijan, your (sg.) husband - 27

kicajuimuwawak, parents [see "nek"] - 54

kichk'hikkau, you (sg.) stay close to him [Ett: 'you must stay near'] - 23

kichki menachgink, near the fence [Ett: no translation] - 23

kichkochqueuch, an unmarried woman - 24

kiegelachchanuk, he makes you (sg.) free [see "Kischellemelang"] - 25

kigawihi, Lend me. (you/sg.) [see "k'payachhican"] - 31

kigeéhellachk; giigeehelachk, your (sg.) physician [lit., 'one who heals you (sg.)] - 14/23

kigelichpenno, an industrious man [Ett: "-pennoe" - difficult to read] - 23

kigelichpii, you (sg.) are industrious [Ett: 'an industrious man'] - 23

kigischquike eet nimat N. wum Bethlehem, perhaps my brother N. comes from Bethlehem, today - 23

kijhei, tin [see "luheluteek"] - 39

kikapawinug, unmarried men [Ett: 'an unmarried man'] - 24

kikau lapi, Is he healed again? [Ett: 'Are you healed again?'] - 24

kikawihi, Lend me. (you/sg.) - 24

kikkeij, old [Ett: "hikkeij"] - 17

kikewa, you (sg.) mend in health [dubious - see "metschi"] - 44

kikgaat, your (sg.) leg - 24

kikibisch wischalawo, the chicken is frightened [Ett: 'the hen has layed' - idiomatic?] - 24

killánnu, your (sg.) tongue - 24

kilawossenanall, our (incl.) Indian corn - 59

kiluna eelsijank, what we (incl.) do [Ett: 'we together] - 24

kiluna gennenoostawatimmenna, we (incl.) understand each other - 24

kiluna k'tehennak niskesch, our (incl.) hearts are unclean [thus Ettwein] - 24

kiluna k'tendeneen, we (incl.) are so [Ett: 'von aus selbst begangen'] - 24

kiluna lithehatamankque, if we (incl.) think about it [Ett: no translation] - 12

kiluwa, you (pl.) - 25/56

kiluwa eelsijeek, as you (pl.) do [Ett: no translation] - 12

kiluwa ktallemussihimmo, you (pl.) go away - 51

kimachtak, your (sg.) brothers - 59

kimachtenna, our (incl.) brother - 59

kimachtenna élank, as we (incl.) say to our brother [Ett: 'our brother says'] - 25

kimachtennaanak, our (incl.) brothers - 59

kimachtowoa, your (pl.) brother - 59

kimachtowoawak, your (pl.) brothers - 59
kimat, your (sg.) brother - 59
kimi, secret [Ett: "qimi"] - 69
kinneû, it is sharp - 25
kischâteek, it shines - 25
Kischellemelang, He Who creates us (incl.) [also see "golang-guumgunatsch"] - 15/25
Kischellemelang amimensoop, the Savior was a child [lit., 'our Creator was a child'] - 25
Kischellemelang angellop, the Savior died [lit., 'our Creator died'] - 25
Kischellemelang kehella k'tomaksoop, our Creator was poor, indeed - 25
Kischellemelang kiegelachchanuk(ch), our Creator will make you (sg.) free [Ett: '... will make me free'] - 25
Kischellemelang k'Patamawosina k'tahoalcuna, our Creator, God in Heaven, loves us (incl.) [lit., 'our Creator, our God, loves us (incl.) - Ett: "-elang Patamawosina k'tahoacuna"] - 26
Kischellemelang k'taholok, our Creator loves you (sg.) - 25
Kischellemelang küschichpatton k'tehenna, the Savior washes our hearts clean [lit., 'our Creator ...'] - 26
Kischellemelang küwingi miwottamaguna, the Savior willingly forgives us (incl.) [Ett: "-melank wingi ..."] - 26
Kischellemelang moocum sogahaleep hakko, the Savior has shed his blood [? "hakkink"] [lit., 'our Creator shed his blood on the ground'] - 26
Kischellemelang wulachenáwall, our Creator sets him loose [Ett: 'the Savior makes me free'] - 25
Kischellemelangcup miwoatamaguna machtschilissowoag-annenanall, the Savior forgives our sins [lit., 'He Who Created us' ...] - 26
Kischelemelanggunk, in the Lord [see "achpiil"] - 1
Kischellemijan, my Creator [lit., 'You Who created me'] - 26
kischélëntamen, he creates it [Ett: 'schaffen (?)'] - 26
kischillemsk'schemsa, Have you (sg.) washed your hands? [Ett: "-emk'schem-"] - 26
kischkingquel woak k'toon, your (sg.) eyes and your (sg.) mouth - 26

kischkschascoagan, a scythe - 26
kischku, a day; it is a day [see "gutte" & "kwawaatoon" & "theu" - Ett: "küschku" once on 36] - 16/36/36/74
kischuch (inan.), month [see "machtschi"] - 41
kischuch (anim.), Sun; Moon [see "metschi" & "usikan"] - 45/77
kischuch kschassum, the Sun burns - 27
kischuch uussiikan, the Sun sets [Ett: 'the Sun is under'] - 27
kischuchchochki, month - 27
kischuésu, he is warm [see "ki"] - 24
kischuweuch, it is warm [Ett: 'warm (in the pew)' - 'warm (in das Stule)'] - 27
kischwê wíquam, the house is warm - 27
kitandschitáwi, make it right - 23
kitschiwi, truly [see "kehella"] - 22
kitschiwi kehella leuch, it is certainly true - 27
klachhican, a trap - 27
klammapi, Sit still. (you/sg.) - 27
klennamawineen, Hold us. (you/sg.) - 27
klenniil, Hold me. (you/sg.) - 27
k'lennilúwi, I do not hold you (sg.) [see "atta"] - 5
k'liichponiwowi, you (sg.) are diligent [thus Ettwein - one might expect k'liilch-] - 22
klitau, fruit - 27
klupijan, you (sg.) turn around [Ett: 'turn over a new leaf' - 'wende das Blat um'] - 27
klussi, you (sg.) will burn yourself - 28
k'magenaniwi, Haven't you (sg.) had time? [see "atta"] - 5
k'mahallumaken, Have you (sg.) bought it? - 28
k'majawina, you (sg.) are right [thus Ettwein - see "jukke"] - 19
kmakáque, Do you (sg.) have the croup? - 28
k'mamawoan, your (sg.) eyebrow - 28
k'manggiechsij, you (sg.) shout [Ett: "-ieschij"] - 28
k'matschalla choeij, you (sg.) bring home a pelt [Ett: "-allach" and 'Go bring the skin here.'] - 28
k'matschewalehenna mattachónel, we (incl.) go for wood - 28
k'matschi, you (sg.) go home [see "metschi"] - 44
k'mauwi [same as "kemauwi"]

k'mecamósij, Do you (sg.) work? - 28

k'mechannessiwi, Aren't you (sg.) ashamed of yourself? [see "atta"] - 4

k'metsche tendehossij, Did you make a fire under the kettle, already? - 28

kmilani, you (sg.) give it to me [one might expect "k'mili" - see "kecu"] - 30

k'mischschamsa, you (sg.) have gotten it [see "kattschi"] - 20

k'miwoatammawij, you (sg.) forgive me [Ett: 'you can forgive me'] - 28

k'miwotamaguna, he forgives us (in.) [Ett: 'you forgive us'] - 28

k'miwotamaguwoa, he forgives you (pl.) [Ett: 'you forgive us'] - 28

k'mochkammen, Have you (sg.) found it? [also see "kpachk-schican"] - 28/31

k'moocummak, your (sg.) veins - 28

k'mócumink, in your (sg.) blood [see "untschi"] - 77

knachchauuschum pawiuch, Is your (sg.) wife pregnant? - 29

knatamen m'bij, you (sg.) fetch water - 29

k'nattenummeneep, you (sg.) took it - 29

knechhua, Are you (sg.) alone? - 29

knennámen jun, Do you (sg.) know this? - 29

knennauwoa lenno, Do you (sg.) know this man? [Ett: "knen-nawiwoa ..."] - 29

knennawoawuna, Do we (in.) know hm? [Ett: 'Do you ..."] - 29

kneta aam anhauwi, Can you (sg.) pay? - 29

kneta ooschuwil(ch), Can you (sg.) swim? - 29

kneta pachkgappehumessijton, Can you (sg.) let blood? [Ett: "... -essijt"] - 29

knewahump, you (sg.) saw him - 56

knewauchsa attuch, Have you (sg.) seen a deer? - 29

knewoawoa, you (pl.) see him - 56

knipawihemenaagup, we (incl.) stood - 60

knipawihump, you (sg.) stood - 60

knitawi sakham, Do you (sg.) have an earring? [lit., 'Can you (sg.) wear an earring?'] - 29

knitschan, your (sg.) child - 29

knuttíke, Do you (sg.) stay at home? - 29

kooch, your (sg.) father [also see "atta" & "nachk'tapu"] - 5/30/48

kookhootit, a little owl - 30

kolachgenimel, I praise you (sg.) [Ett: "-geminel"] - 30

kolachgenimelenneen, we praise you - 30

kolakucheenhummo, I wish you (pl.) a good evening — [Ett: "kolach'nhummen" — difficult to read] - 30

kollamalessi, Are you (sg.) in good health? [Ett: "-essu"] - 30

kowingi lihellen [same as "küwingi lihellen"]

k'pa; k'paah, you (sg.) come [also see "tschinggetsch"] - 46/75

kpachkschican golhattu, Do you (sg.) have your (sg.) knife? - 31

kpachkschican kmochkamen, Have you (sg.) found your (sg.) knife? - 31

k'paah [see "k'pa"]

k'pahemmo; kpahemmoh, you (pl.) come - 31/46

kpahîj, Close it. (you/sg.) [Ett: 'Close the door.'] - 31

kpahij isquandei, Close the door. (you/sg.) - 31

k'pakgamma, you (sg.) hit him - 62

k'pakgamaawo, you (pl.) hit him [Ett: "pak-"] - 62

kpallho, you (sg.) missed him [i.e., 'missed shooting him'] - 31

kpallitoon, you (sg.) do it wrongly [Ett: 'thu es weg'] - 31

k'paalsi, Are you (sg.) sick?; you are sick [Ett: "k'paalsu" at 31] - 31/46

k'palsihimmo, you (pl.) are sick [Ett: "k'palsä-"] - 46

k'paamse, you (sg.) have come [see "kattschi"] - 20

kpaamsihemmenna, we (incl.) are walking [see "anink"] - 4

kpassoweû, deny [thus Ettwein — probably, "kpassowen" & 'you (sg.) deny it'] - 31

kpasukquin, you (sg.) stand up [Ett: "kpasukquon" & 'Stand up.' (you/sg.) - 31

kPatamawosina, our (incl.) God [see "Kischellemelang"] - 26

kpatamel milli, I pray you, give it to me. - 31

k'patten, it is frozen [see "weemi"] - 79

k'payachkhican kigawihi, Lend me your (sg.) gun. [Ett: "k'payachhican"] (you/sg.) - 31

kpayachkhikan, your (sg.) gun [Ett: "kpayachhikan" - see "kecu"] - 30

kpechiwigul, I live close to you (sg.) [Ett: 'you are near'] - 31

34

kpendawa Lenaape, Do you (sg.) understand Indian? [Ett: "kpendawe"] - 32

kpendawi, Do you (sg.) understand me? [Ett: "kpendawe"] - 32

kpendawihump, you (sg.) understood me [Ett: 'you understood him' - see "metschi"] - 44

kpendolowi, I don't understand you (sg.) [see "atta"] - 6

kpeschutineen, we (incl.) have brought it [? 'we bring each other'] - 32

kpettschéwak, they are foolish [Ett: 'they are fools'] - 32

k'saaki, long you [see "tatsch"] - 73

ksakímajemmenna, our (incl.) king - 32

kschachhan, wind [see "machheu" & "ta"] - 43/73

kschachhenn, wind - 32

kschachhenn theu, the wind is cold - 32

kschassum, he burns (something) [see "kischuch"] - 27

kschehélal hoosch, Hang up the kettle. (you/sg.) - 32

kschéton, your (sg.) lip - 32

kschichheek, it is pure - 32

kschichhican, a comb - 32

kschichhíke, I am finished with it - 32

kschichsu, he is pure - 32

kschichtoon, to wash it - 32

kschiechtauwihan, to wash ourselves [thus Ettwein] - 32

kschihâkikhamen, Are you (sg.) drawing lines? - 32

kschihemsake, to wash a shirt [(?) "kschihembsake"] - 32

kschiheesowe, to wash out - 32

k'schilemsk'schemsa, Have you (sg.) washed your hands? [see "keschingquemsaa"] - 23

kschinggala, you (sg.) hate him - 32

kschinggaläwok, you (sg.) hate them - 32

kschinggalell, I hate you (sg.) - 32

kschinggaalguuna, he hates us - 32

kschinggali, you (sg.) hate me - 32

kschinggalihenna, you hate us - 32

kschinggaaluk, he hates you (sg.) - 32

k'schiis, your (sg.) uncle - 62

k'schísenna, our (incl.) uncle - 62

k'schisenanak, our (incl.) uncles - 62

kschisu, he is pure [see "kepe"] - 21

k'schisuuwa, your (pl.) uncle - 62

k'schisuwoawak, your (pl.) uncles - 62

kschittêu, it is hot (food) - 33

kschiwilawelohump, I grieved you (sg.) - 33

kschiwoondican, your (sg.) tobacco pouch - 33

ksinachpílet, you (sg.) are indifferent [thus Ettwein] - 33

ksinachpo, he is at leisure [Ett: 'aufsatzig'] - 33

ksínaaquot, it is dry (cannot sweat) [Ett: 'dry (cannot sweat)' — must refer to some particular inanimate body part] - 33

ksinhatténamo, he is indifferent [Ett: 'du hast was gleich-gultigs'] - 33

ksinhattenamoagan, indifference - 33

ksitink, at your feet [see "gollemikitolenk"] - 15

kta, you (sg.) go [see "na" & "ta"] - 48/72

k'tahoalcuna; k'tahoalguna, he loves us (incl.) [Ett: 'he, you love us' - also see "Kischellemelang"] - 26/33

k'tahoalel ki, I love you (sg.) [Ett: "n'ta-"] - 60

ktahoalell, I love you (sg.) [Ett: "ktahoalelel" / see "abtschi"] - 1

ktahoalenna, we (incl.) love him [see "necama"] - 1

k'tahoaltowoagan, your (sg.) love [see "milineen"] - 47

k'taholgunok, he loves us (incl.) [see "Jesus"] - 18

k'tahooli, you (sg.) love me - 33

k'tahoolillel, I love you (sg.) [dubious] - 33

k'taholok, he loves you (sg.) [see "Kischellemelang"] - 25

k'taholtihennetsch, we (incl.) will love one another - 33

k'tahowaalohump, I loved you (sg.) [see "ni"] - 59

ktahowoali? Do you (sg.) love me? - 1

k'tahowoaluk? Does he love you (sg.)? - 1

ktai'gennenaanak, our (incl.) things (anim.) [Ett: 'to you/it belongs to us' - cp. "tahicana"] - 34

ktajenden, you are so [see "ta"] - 72

ktakpau, it is moist [see "na"] - 48

k'tallamusca, you (sg.) go away [see "tschinggetsch"] - 75

k'tallemussi, you (sg.) go away - 51

k'tallemussihimmo, you (pl.) go away [see "kiluwa"] - 51

k'tallitoon, you (sg.) make it; you (sg.) make them [see "ki"] - 24

k'tallûhumullen, I will teach you (sg.) - 34

k'tamemens, your (sg.) child - 3

k'tamemensemak, your (sg.) children - 3

k'tamemensemennaanak, our (incl.) children - 3

k'tamemensemewoawak, your (pl.) children - 3

ktannes, your (sg.) daughter - 34
k'tangkamuk, he stings you (sg.) [see "aamüwe"] - 4
ktapulchquollana, you (sg.) hold him upside down [Ett: 'upside down'] - 34
ktapúsij, Do you (sg.) roast something? - 34
k'taschewewüchêenna, we (incl.) meet [Ett: 'meet'] - 34
ktayábtoon, you (sg.) talk [see "ki"] - 24
k'te; k'tê, your (sg.) heart [see "kepe" and "k'de"] - 21/21/24
k'tee angeln; k'te angeln, your (sg.) heart is dead - 24/34
k'tehenna, our (incl.) hearts [see "Kischellemelang"] - 26
k'tehennanak, our (incl.) hearts [see "kiluna"] - 24
k'tehowa, your (pl.) hearts - 23
k'tehuwawak, your (pl.) hearts - 34
k'tehuwoawall, your (pl.) hearts [obv.] - 34
k'tehuwoawoawuna, our (incl.) hearts [Impossible! See "k'tehennanak"] - 34
k'tehuwoawunk, in your (pl.) hearts - 34
k'tellan, you (sg.) tell him - 52
k'tellaneen, we (incl.) tell him - 52
k'tellanéwo, you (pl.) tell him - 52
k'tellapewoagan, your (sg.) conscience [Ett: 'the conscience'] - 35
ktellauchsa lapi páme Joh., You (sg.) have said to him, "Come (fut. imp.) again, John." [Ett: 'I have said to you, "Come again soon, John."'] - 35
ktellauchsa métschi N., Have you told N., already? - 35
ktellgemsa N. lapi pame., You (sg.) have been told, N., "Come (fut. imp.) again." [Ett: 'I say to you, "Come again soon."'] - 35
k'telli, you (sg.) thus [Ett: 'you are thus'] - 74
ktellichton, you establish it [see "kecu"] - 30
ktellihellen, I do it to you (sg.) [Ett: 'he will do it'] - 35
ktellíneen, you (sg.) said to us - 35
k'tellohump, I have said it to you (sg.) - 23
k'tellsettawan, you (sg.) listen to him [see "aween"] - 8
ktellungquam, you (sg.) dream - 35
k'temagauchsoágan, a poor, miserable life [see "necama"] - 53
k'temakkelemineen, Pity us. (you/sg.) - 35
ktemaksoop, he was poor [Ett: 'are poor'] - 35
ktendanéwo, you (pl.) do so [see "ta"] - 72

k'tendeneen, we (incl.) are so [see "kiluna"] - 24

kteenhalguna, he redeems us (incl.) [Ett: "-haguna" & 'redeemer'] - 34

kteppimizi, Have you (sg.) eaten enough? [Ett: "ktappi mizi"] - 34

k'tomaksoop, he was poor [see "Kischellemelang"] - 25

k'toon, your (sg.) mouth [see "kischkingquel"] - 26

ktschannitussij, you (sg.) are confused - 35

k'tschihilleuch, it hangs down [see "gaakun"] - 13

ktschinggaluk, he hates you (sg.) [Ett: '? ist m. feind'] - 35

ktschitanîtawi nachkall, you (sg.) strengthen my hands [Ett: "kschi-" & 'you make your hands strong'] - 33

ktschitschangkunanall, our (incl.) souls (obv.) - 35

ktscholtik, Come out, the lot of you. [Ett: "kschol-" & 'Do you come out of school?'] - 33

kudukkiil, Turn around. (you/sg.) - 35

kulalawoasi, you warm yourself well [Ett: 'here (is a good fire) you can warm up good'] - 36

kulelendamen, Are you (sg.) glad? - 36

kulelensowoagan, your (sg.) self-pride [Ett: 'your finery'] - 36

kuleu, it flames [Ett: 'to flame'] - 36

kulichsin, you (sg.) speak well [see "kella"] - 22

kulituwon, you (sg.) have not made it well [see "atta"] - 6

kumen, you come from [see "ta"] - 73

kuppaschkhammen, to stop [i.e., 'to plug'] - 36

kusámi allachpichsi, you (sg.) talk too fast - 36

kuscháteij, tobacco - 36

küschichpatton, he washes it; he washes them (inan.) [see "Kischellemelang"] - 26

küwingi, willingly-us (incl.) [see "Kischellemelang"] - 26

küwingi endeneep, Were you (sg.) so, willingly? [Ett: 'Hast dus gern geschan'] - 36

küwingi lihellen; **kowingi lihellen**, I gladly do it for you (sg.) [Ett: 'Thust dus gern' & "nowingi ..." at 61] - 36/61

küwingi witschéwul, I go with you (sg.) willingly [Ett: "quwingi ..."] - 70

kuwitschewulen, I will go with you (sg.) [Ett: "n'kuwitsch-"] - 60

kwawaatoon mechheek kischku, you (sg.) know it is a great day - 36

kwikameln, I will visit you (sg.) [see "phieteet"] - 67
kwiikeu, he visits [Ett: 'to visit'] - 36
k'wíkhe, you (sg.) build a house [see "tschingetsch"] - 76
kwiwall, your (sg.) wife [see "ki"] — 24

-L-

lahlhägóhcan, a drawing knife - 37
lalíche, the breath - 37
lallogeuch, he works it [see "kecu"] - 30
laalpak; lalpak, to weep; he cries [also see "niank"] - 37/58
langgan, light [i.e., 'light-weight'] - 37
laapi; lapi, again [see "elemegisquik" & "kikau" & "ktel-lauchsa" & "ktellgemsa" & "necama" & "nechog-oniechinoop" & "tschinggetsch"] - 12/24/35/35/ 53/54/75/75
lapi amüíp, he rose again [Ett: 'rose again'] - 37
lappi pommauchsu, Does he live again? - 37
latquehául, he is guilty - 37
lawachtowoagan, price [Ett: "?"] - 37
lawoapanne jukke, now there is broad daylight [Ett: "junke ..."] - 37
lawelakkey, highest grade - 37
lawellentam, he is embarassed [Ett: 'embarassed'] - 37
lawewoagan, something torn - 37
lawié, the middle - 37
l'chachi, loose - 37
lechchauwelemineen, Care for us. (you/sg.) [see "abtschi"] - 1
lechewan, the breath - 37
lekau, sand - 37
lekhamen, to write it - 37
lekhásu, it is written - 37
lekhike, write - 37
lekhiquâtejeku, broad - 38
lelawih, the mid point - 38
lelchlawalujek, a fork - 37
lellenéwo, I say to you (pl.) [conjectural - Ett: 'gesagt'] - 38
lematschi, I go home - 38
lenapandicu, a rear gunsight [see "mallenítu"] - 42
Lenappe; Lenaape; Lennappe, an Indian; Indian (language) [also see "itspiê" & "kpendawa"] - 18/32/38

Lenapewak, Indians [see "n'giwikkaman"] - 58

Lennappewinenk, among the Indians [see "m'piwechineentsch" & "n'tentalineentsch"] - 38/38

lennemmawan, to do it for him [Ett: 'thun' - perhaps, 'to hand
it to him'] - 38

lengtêu, it melts [Ett: 'to melt'] - 38

lenni, Do it. (you/sg.) [see "jul"] - 19

lennito, a little while [see "pechó"] - 66

lenno, a man [also see "knennau" & "machelensu" & "pschiki"
& "tangeto" & "wulilessiit"] - 29/38/40/68/73/83

lenschkanall, fingers - 38

lennuwehellêü, a male bird [Ett: 'a cock'] - 38

lenny, instantly [see "kensch"] - 22

lépaacu, to cry - 38

lëpakguwinaxu, he looks tearful [Ett: 'tearful'] - 38

leppewoacan, knowledge - 38

léu; leuch, it is true [see "kehella" & "kitschiwi" & "kecu" &
"nanne" & "ta] - 22/22/27/30/49/72

lewi, it is not true [see "atta"] - 6

lewonneen, it is possible [see "heekee"] - 17

lhillpennewoagan, willingness - 38

liechsiáne, if I speak [see "a"] - 2

liechsin, speak [see "n'gatta'] - 57

lihellen, I do it for you (sg.) [see "kowingi" & "küwingi"]
- 36/61

lihineen, Do it for us. (you/sg.) [Ett: 'Do it.'] - 38

lij, to say [see "kemauwi"] - 28

likiihillaaneen, we flourish [Ett: 'Let us flourish.'] - 38

lilligpi, I am willing ["g" = "ch" - Ett: 'willing'] - 38

limattupe nimat, Sit down, my brother. - 38

lissian, you (sg.) do something [see "quatsch"] - 69

lissinen, we do it [see "kehella"] - 22

litehamáte, if he thinks about it [Ett: 'What do you think?;
when we think'] - 38

liteháwak, they think about it [see "atta"] - 5

lithehatamankque, if we (incl.) think about it [see "kiluna"]
- 12

litthewi, does not think about it [see "necama"] - 53

lkacal, basket wood [i.e., 'splints'- Ett: 'Korbe holz'] {as per
JR} - 38

l'likhikquegen, so as [conjectural - Ett: '(Er) ists ?'] - 38

lócam, meal - 38

lócat, meal - 38

lochwatol, Carry it along. (you/sg.) - 38

loogat, flour [see "ta"] - 73

loghammen, to pull something over {as per JR} - 39

logkihilleu, it tears [i.e., 'it rips'] - 39

loltik, Come out. (the lot of you) [see "wikwahemink"] - 80

looquejánne, when he tells you (sg.) [Ett: 'when I say it'] - 39

lowonsu, he is named [see "kecu"] - 30

luêuch, he says - 39

luéwak, they say [also see "nik"] - 39/59

luheluteek kijhei, tin - 39

luhikan, pointer finger [i.e., 'index finger' - cp. "joheka"] - 39

luhumelen, I teach (you/sg.) [see "katta"] - 20

lúhwonge, when it is Winter [Ett: 'in Winter'] - 39

lukuun, he tells (you) [see "kemauwi"] - 28

lume, Tell him. (you/sg.) [fut.imp. - Ett: 'Command.'] - 39

lussahican, a foot-rule - 39

lussin, to burn [Ett: 'burnt'] - 39

lussiwi, I am not burnt [see "atta"] - 7

lutéke, when it burns [Ett: 'it burns'] - 39

luwann, Winter - 39

luwanneung wundachen, it comes from the North [Ett: '... northwest'] - 39

luwe, Say it. (you/sg.) [see "tschitsch"] — 76

-M-

mâ, in the past [past tense marker - see "mikemossijaane"] - 47

machchaaptonágat ijoon aptonacan jukke gischquik, this word is a great word, today [Ett: 'heute heissen die grosse Worte'] - 39

machchaquichen sipung, the stream is very deep [lit., 'it is very deep in the stream'] - 39

machascútscheu, he is thick-bellied [Ett: 'dicken bauch'] - 39

machelendammen, to esteem it [Ett: 'es ist ?'] - 39

machelensowoagan, haughtiness [Ett: "machhel-"] - 40

mächelensijte, if he is haughty [Ett: "mächh-" & 'haughty'] - 43

machelensu lenno, a haughty man - 40
machcheli, many - 40
machcheli pekok, many wounds [i.e., 'many holes' - Ett: "machheli"] - 40
machchelook, many (this is used for animate things) - 40
machchilawewoagan, a big hunt - 40
machgáchqual, pumpkins - 40
machhaket lenno, a big man - 40
machhéken; machhiken, animal hair; hair - 40/43
mächhêu, it is great - 43
machheu kschachhan, a great wind [Ett: "machhau"] - 43
machkakenema, exalt; praise - 39
machkeu, it is red - 40
machksumen, to dye it red [Ett: 'dyed'] - 40
machquik(ch), there are many bears - 40
machquiin; machquin, it is swollen [see "nehikgaat" & "nootschque"] - 54/54
machquing, it swells [see "natschque"] - 50
machtakeen, to fight - 40
machtakewak, they fight [Ett: 'enemy'] - 40
machtapach, war [one might expect "machtapeek"] - 40
machtetsu elaloge, it is badly made [Ett: 'you (sg.) have made something bad'] - 40
machtissu, he is ugly; he is useless - 41
machtógat, a grave - 40
machtschi kischuch, a bad month - 41
machtschi m'tächen, bad wood (sg.) [cp. "matachen"] - 41
machtschijei, a grave - 41
machtschijejall, graves - 41
machtschiwindasu, it is badly translated [Ett: 'he has ...'] - 41
macschawik, trifolium with the red flowers - 43
maganapiwij, I don't have time [see "atta"] - 6
mahallammen; mahallamen, to buy it [Ett: 'I buy' on 41] - 20/41
mahallas, flint stone - 41
mahokquame, ice - 41
máhholohla, send [see "ni"] - 59
majauchso nochenna, our (ex.) one father [Ett: 'one father'] - 41
majawi, proper [Ett: 'wahres'] - 41
makamene, leave [see "kattschi"] - 20

makial, a rash - 41

makij, a scab - 41

makiktschewa, a groundhog [cp., Ett: 'grund dap' & Zeis: 'grund-tap'] - 41

mallachcüsitall, beans - 41

mallenítu, he makes it [Ett: 'we make'] - 42

mallenitu hokappehellat, he makes a decorative trim piece [i.e., for a rifle] [Ett: '... eine garnetur'] - 42

mallenítu huiktschi, he makes a breech screw [Ett: '... eine Schw. Schraube'] - 42

mallenítu lenapandicu, he makes a rear gunsight [Ett: '... ein Visir'] - 42

mallenítu mechámet, he makes a hammer spring' [Ett: '... eine Schlag feder' — part of the gunlock mechanism] - 42

mallenítu penthicana ehellamuik, he makes a ramrod holder [i.e., the handle under the barrel which holds the ramrod - Ett: '... Heft'] - 42

mallenítu tschicócan, he makes a scraper [i.e., 'a fouling scraper' - Ett: '... einen Kratzer'] - 42

mallenítu w'siitak(ch), he makes a gunstock [Ett: '... ein Schaft der Flinte'] - 42

malennituwon, not make it [see "atta"] - 6

malowencu, whoring - 42

mamáwad, an eyebrow [dubious - one would expect "mamáwan" {as per JR}] - 42

mameelandamën, to vomit [Ett: 'he vomits'] - 42

mamelandammoop, he vomited - 42

mamki, pimply [conjectural rendering - Ett: no translation] {as per JR} - 42

maamschálime, Remember me. (you/sg.) [fut.imp.] - 42

mammukcowoagan, destruction [Ett: no translation] - 42

manakquon, a rainbow - 42

maníhtu, he makes it [Ett: "maníhte" & 'we make'] - 42

maníhtu ehamhitehúkkuk, he makes the battery [i.e., 'the frizzen' - Ett: '... battri' — part of the gunlock mechanism] - 42

maníhtu kandschoctican, he makes the flashpan [Ett: '... die Pfanne'] - 42

maníhtu matagunihcan, he makes the sear [Ett: '... das Senget' — part of the gunlock mechanism] - 42

maníhtu mematschéhella, he makes the cock [i.e., 'the hammer' - Ett: '... der Hahn' — part of the gunlock mechanism] - 42

manittuwak, they make it [see "kecu"] - 30

manschawinaku hubwoagan, the tobacco pipe looks very fine [Ett: "manschawunaku"] - 43

manunginaaxu, he looks angry [Ett: 'er sieht z. aus'] - 42

manungsu, he is angry - 42

manungsuwoagan, anger - 42

maschanin, the stinging nettle - 43

maskíquoll, grass - 43

matachen, wood (sg.) [see "nemetschi" - cp. "machtschi m'tächen"] - 55

mattachónel; matachonall, wood (pl.) [also see "k'matschewalehummenna"] - 28/41

matagunihcan, a sear [see "maníhtu" — part of the gunlock mechanism] - 42

matapasican, poison - 43

mattauchsowoagan, sin - 43

matemeeke; mattemeeke, Come in. (you/sg.) [Ett: 'Take it' on p.44] - 43/44

matscheuch, he goes home [see "tschinge"] - 75

matschi, go home [see "ni"] - 59

mátschil, Go home. (you/sg.) - 41

matschimaquat, it stinks - 41

mattschitam, Let us go home. [see "juchta"] - 18

matumme, a wolf [see "tatta"] - 73

mauallawi, go hunting [see "n'tachquache"] - 63

mauchsu, one (anim.) [Ett: "maugsu"] - 43

mawewin, there is an assembly [Ett: 'versammlung'] - 42

mawewink, an assembly - 42

mawikatam, Let us camp. [Ett: 'Where shall we camp?'] - 43

m'bechowe, I wait [Ett: "m'bechow"] - 46

m'bij, water [Ett: "m'bii" on 45 - also see "knatamen"] - 29/45

m'bij natamen, I fetch water - 45

m'bijachku, a whale - 45

m'dukschummen, to wound by cutting - 45

mecamoosy, work [i.e., "mikemossi" - see "nowingi"] - 61

mechámet, a hammer spring [see "mallenítu" — part of the gunlock mechanism] - 42

mechheek, that which is great; big [see "kwawaatoon" & "tatta"] - 36/73

mechhek elalogunk, a miracle; a great work [Ett: '?'] - 43

mechhiechsij, Speak loudly. (you/sg.) [Ett: "mechhechsij"] - 43

mejawillseet lenno, a God-fearing man - 43

mekindamen, work it [see "kecu" - cp. "migentamool"] - 31

mematschéhella, a cock; a hammer [also see "manîhtu" — part of the gunlock mechanism] - 42/43

memenachpiitschik, congregation [lit., 'they who repeatedly sit together' - [Ett: 'gemeine'] - 43

menachgink, on the fence [see "kichki"] - 23

menachpijank, we (incl.) sit together - 43

menahee, Give me something to drink. (you/sg.) - 43

menne, drink [see "nemetschi"] - 55

menneel, Drink. (you/sg.) - 44

menneluk, a pile [see "n'gutte"] - 58

mennéu, he drinks [see "wusami"] - 84

mequit, bloody - 44

mesall, his older sister [see "necama"] - 53

meschaltienke, when we (ex.) remember one another [Ett; 'Have you (sg.) remembered him?'] - 44

messenawak, captives - 44

messissu, it is whole - 44

meetennáxit, he is ready - 44

meetschi; metschi, already [Ett: "metsche" at 25 - also see "ki" & "ktellauchsa"] - 25/35/60

metschi amíhillëu, it is already fallen down - 44

metschi khíke, Are you (sg.) healed, already? - 44

metschi khikëunge, they (abv.) are healed, already - 44

metschi kikewa, Are you (sg.) healing, already? [dubious - thus Ettwein] - 44

metschi k'matschi, Are you (sg.) going home, already? - 44

metschi kpendawihump, Did you (sg.) understand me, already? [Ett: 'Did you understand him, rightly?'] - 44

metschi milan, he gave it to him, already [Ett: 'have given'] - 44

metschi notalauwi, I have already begun to hunt - 45

metschi nutalóge, I have already begun to work [Ett: 'I have begun'] - 45

metschi nutenakuak, they have already begun - 45

metschi nutschi alletol, they (inan.) have already begun to rot - 45

metschi nutschi pauwîhillewoll, they have already begun to fall [Ett: 'they begin to fall in Winter'] - 45

metschi paachhakque, it is already midday - 45

metschi paw kischuch, the Sun comes up, already; the Moon comes up, already [(?) paw = peu] - 45

metschi sokennupaalittschik, they who are already baptized [Ett: 'the baptized'] - 45

metschihilleu, it is ragged - 44

meyentammennépanni, he took our sins unto himself [thus Ettwein] - 43

m'hittapitup, he was born [Ett: "-pitip" & 'first born'] - 45

m'hittgunk, on a tree [see "aschtetehasik"] - 4

m'hitquapapun, a wicker chair - 46

m'hittschiju, it (anim.) is barren - 46

m'hittuck, a tree [see "husca"] - 18

michapoonen, eyelid - 46

michasquel, grass - 46

micoon [see "mikon"]

migentamool, I work for (you/sg.) [see "gëmauwi" - cp. "mekindamen"] - 14

mihilussiwi, is not old [see "atta"] - 6

mikeemossiechtítte, if they work - 47

mikeemossijaane, if I work [Ett: "-iaane"] - 47

mikemossijaane mâ, if I worked (etc. & so forth, but mâ on the end) [i.e., add "mâ" to each form of "mikemossi-" to make the perfect tense, as with this one] - 47

mikeemossijanne, if you (sg.) work - 47

mikemossijannetsch, if you (sg.) will work [Ett: no translation, but notes 'future' - i.e., 'future tense.'] - 47

mikeemossijankque, if we (incl.) work - 47

mikeemossijeekque, if you (pl.) work - 47

mikeemossítte, if he works - 47

mikon; miccoon, a quill; a feather [also see "ehellekikehond"] - 11/46

milaak, hair - 46

milak(ch), he doesn't give it to him [Ett: 'Give.'] - 46

millamaquat, it smells [Ett: 'the smell'] - 46

milan, he gives it to him [see "metschi"] - 44

milanéwo, they give it to him [Ett: "-éwe" & 'they give'] - 46

milank, we give it to him [see "atta"] - 6

milate; milaate, if he gives it to him [Ett: 'if we give'] - 46/46

milawat, Didn't you (sg.) give it to him? [Ett: 'Do you (sg.) give?'] - 46

milawécü, Didn't you (pl.) give it to him? [Ett: 'Do you (sg.) give?'] - 46

mili; milli, Give it to me. (you/sg.) [see "kecheti" & "kpa-tamel" & "N."] - 21/31/43

mili jun, Give me this. (you/sg.) - 47

mili nemitschin kecu, Give me something to eat. (you/sg.) - 47

miliégetsch, Don't give it to him. (you/sg.) [see "kattschi"] - 20

milíneen, Give it to us. (you/sg.) - 46

milineen k'tahoaltowoagan, Give us your (sg.) love. (you/sg.) [Ett: 'Let us into your love.'] - 47

milineen wulantowoagan, Give us grace. (you/sg.) - 47

milkuneen, he gives it to us [Ett: 'grant us'] - 47

mingachsa peki, somewhat better sometimes [Ett: 'etwas besser zuweilen'] - 47

mingku, seed - 47

mitschijeksa, you (pl.) have eaten it [see "kecu"] - 31

miwoatammawíneen, Forgive us. (you/sg.) - 47

miwottamaguna; miwoatamaguna, he forgives them (inan.) for us [see "Kischellemelang" & "Kischellemelangcup"] - 26

mizowoagan; mizoagan, food; provisions; victuals [also see "n'gennimmen"] - 47/47/57

mochhican, a lock [see "n'gatta"] - 57

moocum, his blood [Ett: 'blood' on 47 - also see "Kischellemelang" & "ni"] - 26/47/60/60

mohoccu, blood [see "ki"] - 25

moschhakquat, it clears up [i.e., the weather] - 47

mootsch, atonement [see "jukke"] - 19

m'pa, I come - 46

m'pahemmenna, we (ex.) come - 46

m'pahump, I came [Ett: 'perf.' - indicating tense] - 46

m'pajaane, if I come [note prefix on conjunct form, as with some other Moravians] - 46

m'pakgammaap, I did hit him [Ett: 'perf.'] - 62
m'pakgamaawonna, we (ex.) hit him - 62
m'paalsi, I am sick - 46
m'palsihenna, we (ex.) are sick - 46
m'pálsihump, I was sick - 46
m'paneep, I came [Ett: 'perf.' - indicating tense] - 46
m'papemmetonhe, I preach - 51
m'paskochwe, I walk down [Ett: 'come down'] - 44
m'Patamawos, my God [see "nowingi"] - 61
m'pechammaasin, I feed someone - 46
m'pechchuwigamen, I come near - 46
m'pehan, I wait for him - 65
m'pendawatimennah, we (ex.) understand each other [see "niluna"] - 59
m'piwechineentsch Lennappewinenk, I will die among the Indians - 38
m'pummsi, I walk - 46
m'schakaano, wound [i.e., 'sore' - thus Ettwein] - 46
m'tächen, wood (sg.) [see "machtschi" - cp. "matachen"] - 41
m'tachen wullit, the wood is good - 46
m'tachinall, wood (pl.) [see "najunta"] - 49
m'tschitschang(ch), a spirit [see "Weelsit"] - 79
m'tschitschangkwall, someone's soul (obv.) [Ett: 'his soul'] - 46
muchgaminesa, he has found it [Ett: "mach-"] - 40
muchkammen, to find [Ett: 'gefunden'] - 47
muchkawi, Kiss me. (you/sg.) - 47
muchkawoaláwall, he kisses him [Ett: "-áwa"] - 47
muschammu, fathom [see "keche"] - 21

-N-

N., N. [see "kigischquike" & "ktellauchsa" & "ktellgemsa" & "nëmachche" & "nemachkawo" & "phieteet" & "ta" & "wunihillatammen" & "wuntschim"] - 23/35/35/54/67/73/84/84
N. aawehellewak, the N's fly away [Ett: 'the N's all fly away'] - 9
N. el mili, Say it, N. Give it to me. (you/sg.) [Ett: 'N. will give it to you'] - 43
N.N., N.N. [see "tschinge"] - 75

N.N. palliku, N.N. suffered an injury - 62

N. nemattamiha, I have lent N. - 49

N. nowitschéjuk, N. goes with me - 49

n', I; me; we (ex.); us (ex.) [prefix] - 56

na, that one (anim.) [see "auween"] - 8

na ju achpiil, Stay here. (you/sg.) [Ett: "najuachpiil" & 'Stay home.'] - 48

na ju talli, there it is [Ett: "naja talli"] - 48

na ju wuntschi wâholomat kehella, yes, it is far from here - 48

na jukke ktakpau hakkij, the ground is moist, at present [Ett: "najukkek kt- ..."] - 48

na k'higauwihuk, he lends that to you (sg.) [Ett: 'you have lent to me'] - 48

na kta, there you (sg.) go [Ett: no translation] - 48

na n'haggelanuima, I trust him [Ett: "naan'ha-"] - 49

nachgooma, I answer him - 48

nachhaasi, Take care. (you/sg.) [Ett: 'innen dich in acht'] - 48

nachk, my hand [Ett: 'a hand'] - 48

nachkall; nachkkal, my hands [also see "ktschitanîtawi"] - 33/48

nachkale, forehead - 48

nachkink, in my hand - 48

nachkohomauwi, Sing. (you/sg.) [Ett: 'Sing a verse.' at 48] - 18/48

nachk'tapu kooch, Is your (sg.) father at home? [Ett: "nach k'tapug kooch"] - 48

nachkumu, he answers - 48

nachóak, they (anim.) are three [see "elitsch"] - 12

nachtuépi, my body - 48

nagajeeke, by and by [Ett: "?"] - 48

nagewiti, a little while [same as "nakkewiti"] - 48

najuum; najum, Carry him. (you/sg.) [i.e., 'on your back' - Ett: 'I carry' & 'carry you'] - 48/49

najuumi, Carry me (on your (sg.) back) [Ett: 'Carry me across.'] - 49

najuumuk, he carries me (on his back) [see "A."] - 49

najunta m'tachinall, Carry the wood. (you/sg.) [i.e., 'on your back'] - 49

najuntam, he carries it (on his back) [see "kecu"] - 49

najuntammen, I carry something on my back [also see "kecu"] - 48/49

nakewi, a little while [see "peuchil"] - 65

nakkewiti paal wikkia, Come to my house, in a little while (you/sg.) [cp. "nagewiti"] - 48

nálambissi, I bind it [Ett: "nálan-"] - 49

namawemizin, I go to eat [see "ni"] - 59

namecamósij, I work [i.e., "n'mikemossi" - see "ni" - cp. "nemecamosij"] - 59

names, a fish [see "n'gattotamen"] - 57

nan, that; that one (anim.) [see "aween" & "nowawaha" & "schi"] - 8/60/87/87

nannachquoméwak, the fish leap - 49

nanne; nane, that (inan.) [see "kehella" & "nen"] - 22/56

nanne, now [thus Ettwein] - 49

nanne leuch, it is surely true - 49

nanne téppi ni, it is enough now for me - 49

nangquan, heel - 49

napäkan, forearm [Ett: 'arm under the elbow'] - 49

nassiti, rear-end (of the body) [Ett: 'rear'] - 49

nasitit, my hip [thus Ettwein] - 49

natta ochquewall, I will take a woman - 49

natta woa amimiwe, I will take this dove - 49

natachtaala, I am also known to him - 49/49

natamen, I fetch it [see "metschi"] - 45

náttchan n'dapoan, that is all my bread [i.e., 'it is all gone'] - 49

nattemmenneep, I fetched it - 50

natemmentsch, I will fetch it - 50

nattenawak, they take him - 50

natenengep, one who carried them (inan.) in his arms [see "schi"] - 87

nattenik, Take me. (you/pl.) - 49

natenniil, Take me. (you/sg.) [Ett: '? mich] - 50

natténnuk, he fetches me - 49

nattennum, I take it - 49

natenummoch, Take it. (you/pl.) [conjectural: reading "-och" as "-ok" - Ett: '?'] - 50

natey, my stomach - 50

Nathaniel, Nathaniel [see "duchwilu"] - 11

nattonamenneen, we seek it - 50

nattonaawa; natonawo, I seek him - 50/50

natonawohump, I sought him - 50
natunammen, to seek - 50
natupäli, I go to war - 50
natschnenen tepelentammen, thus, I will cease ["natschnene n'tepelentammen" pronounced like this] - 50
natschque machquing, it swelled spontaneously - 50
nawe woak wulelendamen, he himself is glad, also [thus Ettwein] - 50
nawechínke, when it is mid-afternoon [Ett: 'um 3. herrum' - 'round about 3 p.m.'] - 50
nawehalláte, when it is mid-afternoon [Ett: 'um 3. herrum' - 'round about 3 p.m.'] - 50
nawipóquat, it tastes good [Ett: 'der geschmack'] - 50
nawochquecu, he hangs down his head [Ett: 'the head hangs'] - 50
nawoquepu, he hangs down his head [Ett: 'the head hangs'] - 50
nawowiganine, I have a backache [Ett: 'my back has an ache'] - 50
n'bumsi, I walk [Ett: no translation] - 59
n'chansa, my older brother [abv.] - 50
n'da waholomi, I go far off - 52
n'dachkoolsi, I conceal it [Ett: "n'achkooli"] - 48
n'dachkolsihenna, we (ex.) conceal it [Ett: no translation] - 48
n'dachquatschi, I am cold [Ett: 'es friert mich'] - 51
n'dah, I go [see "waholomi" & "wuli"] - 78/83
n'dahemmenna, we (ex.) go [see "gamink"] - 13
n'dahn, I go [see "Bethlehem" & "hokkung" & "tatsch"] - 9/17/74
n'dahonukguuk, they take me prisoner - 51
n'dahowoala, I love him [see "necaama"] - 1
n'dajabtoon, I speak; I talk [also see "ni"] - 51/59
n'dajahoeli, I am willful [Ett: 'ich bedarf'] - 51
n'dakkindamen jun, I will read this - 51
n'dallachímen, I rest - 51
n'dallawewe achwoala, I love him more [Ett: 'my dearest'] - 51
n'dallawiin, I go hunting - 51
n'dallemi khikkínammenneen, we (ex.) begin to recognize it [Ett: 'in d. Erkenntnis nehmen zu'] - 51
n'dallemussi, I go away; I will go - 51

n'dallemussihemmena, we (ex.) go away [see "niluna"] - 51
n'dalletonhe, I preach - 51
n'damasktiwij, I cannot defecate [see "atta"] - 6
n'damemensi, I am a child - 53
n'damemensíhummena, we (ex.) are children - 53
n'damemensihummenagup, we (ex.) were children - 53
n'damemensihump, I was a child - 53
n'damemensineep, I was a child - 53
n'dammennemen, Dare I take it? - 51
n'dammuii, I stand up - 51
n'daan, my daughter - 10
n'daanak, my daughters - 10
n'dandlan, I learn [Ett: 'I am a student' - cp. "nhittantelan"]
{as per JR} - 51
n'daanennä, our (ex.) daughter - 10
n'daanennaanak, our (ex.) daughters - 10
n'dannes, my daughter - 51
n'danghillawu, I dishonor him - 51
n'dappi, I stay - 51
n'dappihemenna, we (ex.) stay - 51
n'dappihump, I stayed - 51
n'dappin, I stay; I remain - 51
n'dappinenagup, we (ex.) stayed - 51
n'dappitsch, I will stay here - 51
n'dapoan, my bread [see "náttchan"] - 49
n'daschpochwe, I go up - 52
n'datehammen, I will extinguish it [i.e., 'a fire'] - 52
n'de, my heart [see "niank"] - 58
n'de pommauchsitam, My heart, let us live. [Ett: 'I feel alive
in my heart'] - 53
n'de pommauchsu, my heart is alive - 53
n'dehennanink, in our (ex.) hearts [see "abtschi" & "eelsijank"] - 1/12
n'dehenk talli, in my heart - 52
n'deijennemmen, Dare I take it? - 51
n'dekkeij, my shoulder [Ett: "m'dekkeij"] - 45
n'dellamangan, my upper arm [Ett: 'my arm'] - 52
n'dellan, I tell him - 52
n'dellaanenagup, we (ex.) told him - 52
n'dellaaneep, I told him - 52
n'delangooma, my friend - 52
n'dellaschumen, I shine it [Ett: 'to shine'] - 52

n'dellatschimogaak, I relate it to you (pl.) - 52
n'dellatschimolchuk, he relates it to me - 52
n'dellatschimui, I question something; I relate something - 52
n'dellekhíke, I write [Ett: "-hikëu"] - 52
n'dellenahawan, my right hand [Ett: 'to the right hand'] - 52
n'dellichche, I lie down - 52
n'dellichihinen, we (ex.) lie down - 52
n'delliteha, I think - 52
n'dellitheham, I think of it [see "abtschi"] - 1
n'delliwoaneen, we (ex.) have it legally [Ett: '(was) wir gehort habe das gesetz'] - 52
n'delsettammën, I listen to it - 52
n'delluktawon, I haven't asked you (sg.) [see "atta"] - 6
n'denteúuchen, I make a fire - 52
n'dequaloge, I stop working {as per TMT} - 53
n'dite, for [see "atta"] - 6
n'diteek, I think so, too [thus Ettwein] - 53
n'doon, my mouth - 53
n'duchwilim eet a, I should become a good hunter [Ett: "n'duchwili méta: & 'ich will ein guter Jager werde'] - 53
n'dulhaal, my breast [i.e., 'chest' - one would expect "n'dulheu"] - 53
necama, he; him; she; her - 56
necama allachimen, he rests - 53
necama allemusso, he goes away - 51
necama atta litthewi, he doesn't think about it - 53
necama atta olhattuwi, he doesn't have it - 53
necama eelsit, as he does [Ett: no translation] - 12
necama gechkauwit, his bed [lit., 'where he repeatedly sleeps'] - 53
necama ktahoalenna, we (incl.) love him - 1
necama k'temagauchsoágan, his poor, miserable life [Ett: 'ergibt dir d. Sunden'] - 53
necama lapi paug, he is coming again [one would expect "peu"] - 53
necama mesall, his oldest sister [i.e., 'elder sister'] - 53
necaama n'dahowoala, I love him - 1
necama patamaweuch, he prays - 53
necama wawulelendamën, he is glad - 53

necamawa eelsiechtit, as they do [Ett: no translation] - 12

necamawa w'schisuwoawall, their uncles - 62

nechogoniechinoop lapi amuip, after three days he rose up, again - 54

nechhun, alone [thus Ettwein] - 50

nehikgaat machquin, my leg is swollen - 54

nehillatam, he owns it [Ett: 'kill'] - 54

neichkoot, it is apparent [Ett: "neigkoot" & 'sieht (auge)'] - 54

nejundángep, one who carried them on his back [see "schi"] - 87

nek, those (anim.) [see "wulatenamoak"] - 83

nek kicajuimuwawak, those (are) your (pl.) parents [Ett: 'your parents'] - 54

neek untschi, for their sakes - 54

neelak; nelak, beyond; yonder [see "jetta" & "wundach"] - 18/84

neeli pómmii, while - 54

neliuhóggala, I comfort him; I encourage him [conjectural at 54 - Ett: 'ich sprech ihm muth zu'] - 54/61

neliuhoggaluksi, I am comforted [Ett: "-aluski"] - 61

neliwelendamohalgussij, I am comforted - 54

neliwelendamohóla, I comfort him - 61

nëmachche wittahemuk N., N. helped me a lot - 54

nemachchelendammen, I esteem it [Ett: 'wir aller grosses'] - 54

nemachkawo N., I find N. - 54

nemahallemmenneep, I bought it - 54

nemamatschilaweemke, I have it by experience [thus Ettwein] - 54

nemamelandameen, I vomit [Ett: 'ich breche mich'] - 55

nemamelandammohump, I vomited [thus Ettwein - Ett: "-huml" & 'ich habe mich gebrechen'] - 55

nemamelandamtsch, I will vomit - 55

nemamschalkussowoagan, my memory; my remembrance - 54

nematakkundehemenna, our (ex.) enemy [? 'we (excl.) fight each other'] - 55

nemattamiha, I lend him [see "N."] - 49

nemecamosij, I work [i.e., "n'mikemossi" - cp. "name-camosij"] - 55

nemechannessi, I am ashamed - 55
nemmenneu, I must drink [dubious] - 55
nemenneen, we drink - 55
némenneep, I saw it - 55
nemetenakusiwi, I am not ready [see "nescota"] - 56
nemetschi menne, I already drank - 55
nemetschi pahallamen matachen, I already split the wood - 55
nemetschi tendeuchhen, I already made a fire - 55
nemewoagan, eyesight - 50
nemischawi, I have gotten none [see "atta"] - 6
nemitschin, I eat it [see "mili"] - 47
nemóchkammen, I found it - 55
nemochkawoatamen, I kiss it [Ett: "-waotamen"] - 55
nemuchkawoala, I kiss him - 55
nenn, So! - 50
nen nane éjabtschi, Is that one and the same? - 56
nennanéwoa, I know him - 56
nenchchanipakkak, green clover - 56
nene wikit, this house [lit., 'that is where he lives'] - 56
nenggihilleu, it shakes - 56
nenoostammen, I understand it [also see "atta"] - 6/56
nenoostammenneen, we (ex.) understand it [Ett: '?'] - 56
neschking, my eye - 56
neschkingquell, my eyes - 56
neesco sokenuppassiquik/ch/, the unbaptized [lit., 'they who are not yet baptized'] - 13
nescota kgischenakusiwi, you (sg.) are not yet ready (with the work) [Ett: "nescotak gisch-" & 'I am not ...'] - 56
nescota nemetenakusiwi, I am not yet ready (to go), 56
nescota newewihawi, I do not yet know him [Ett: 'I do not know of it'] - 56
nesgallengü, a Negro - 56
nesgallengüak, Negroes - 56
neskalenkéwinench, a Negro district ["-ch" = "-k," here - lit., 'among the Negroes' - Ett: "niskalenke win-"] - 60
netajaluchka, I work [Ett: 'taja-" & no translation] - 55
neetammi, first [see "ki"] - 25
newaahump, I saw him - 56

newentschi, therefore - 56
newewihawi, I do not know him [see "nescota"] - 56
néwiiquiik, they do not see me [see "nik"] - 56
newoap, I saw him [see "eli"] - 12
newoawonna, we (ex.) see him - 56
newotte, if he saw him - 56
newótsch Jesum, I will see my Jesus - 56
newull, I see (you/sg.) [see "kemauwi"] - 22
n'gakelülük, he calls me a liar - 56
n'gaasumen, I will dry it - 56
n'gatta liechsin eliechsian, I want to speak your (sg.) language
    [lit., 'I want to speak the way you (sg.) speak' - Ett
    first wrote "... alliichsiin elligsian" then "... lechsin
    ..." & 'I wish to know the language'] - 57
n'gatta mochhican, I want a lock - 57
n'gatta ochwee, I want to walk [one might expect "... och-
    ween"] - 57
n'gatta tauwiquocan, I want a key - 57
n'gatta tschikócan, I want a scraper [cp. "tschicocan"] - 57
n'gattam, I would (yes) - 13
n'gattatam, I desire something [Ett: no translation on 57]-
    13/57
n'gattammuwij, I don't want it [Ett: "n'katta-" - see "atta"]
    - 7
n'gattatamen, I want it [Ett: "n'katta-" - see "atta"] - 7
n'gattotamen achpoan, I want bread [i.e., 'to eat' - Ett:
    "n'katto-"] - 60
n'gattotamen names, I want a fish [i.e., 'to eat' - ungrammati-
    cal - TI verb should be TA, "n'gattupwau" - but,
    see Zeisberger's Grammar, p.39, where 'fish' is
    inanimate!] - 57
n'gattumquam, I am sleepy [lit., 'I want to sleep'] - 57
n'gattuupwe, I am hungry [Ett: "-pe" at 57 - also see "kehel-
    la"] - 22/57
n'gattuussaamô, I am thirsty [Ett: "n'kattu-"] - 50
n'gauwi, I sleep - 58
n'gauwihimmena, we (ex.) sleep - 58
n'gauwihump, I slept - 58
n'gauwineep, I slept - 57
n'geegum, my money - 58
n'geegumall, my monies (obv.) - 58

n'geelennemen, I carry something on my arm (or 'in my hand') - 48

n'gennimmen mizowoagan, I will take along provisions [thus Ettwein - perhaps, "n'gelenn-" is meant] - 57

n'geschiechemmokgoop, he washed me - 57

n'geschiechemmoktsch, he will wash me - 57

n'geschiechtoneen, we (ex.) wash it - 57

n'geschietoon, I wash it - 57

n'gessij, I am hot - 57

n'gettamáksij, I am poor - 57 [{as per JR} - Ett: -makij]

n'giescheléchi, I am hot - 57

n'giespwe, I am full [i.e., 'I have had enough to eat' - Ett: "n'giespe"] - 57

n'gikhau, I heal him [Ett: "n'gikau" & 'it heals me'] - 58

n'gikinawo, I am well-acquainted with him - 57

n'gikinawootíhemenna, we are well-acquainted with one another [Ett: '... with him'] - 57

n'gischalooge, I am finished working [Ett: 'I am finished'] - 57

n'giwikkaman Lenapewak, I visit the Indians [Ett: no translation] - 58

n'glisiin, I gird - 58

n'gochgawe, I am under [see "amochchool"] - 3

n'gommawe, constantly [Ett: no translation] - 58

n'gulquechchinen, I sprain myself - 58

n'gusquine, I sneeze - 58

n'gutte menneluk, one pile - 58

n'guttitehewoacan, unity of thought [Ett: 'die Einigkeit oder ?'] - 58

n'gutko, my knee [cp. "n'kátuk"] - 58

n'haggelanuima, I trust him [see "na"] - 49

n'higachquan, my shin bone - 58

n'higasch, my nail [i.e., 'fingernail' or 'toenail'] - 58

n'higaschak, my nails [i.e., 'fingernails' or 'toenails'] - 58

n'hikkiwon, my nose - 58

n'hitta, I could; I can [see "atta"] - 5/6

n'hittammi, at first - 58

n'hittantelan, I will learn [cp. "n'dandlan"] - 58

n'hittawak, my ear - 58

n'hittawakall, my ears [obv.] - 58

n'hittawi, I can - 6

n'hukqui, my chin - 58

nii; ni, I; me; my [also see "niin" & "jukkela" & "nanne" & "weemi"] - 3/49/56/79

ni eholon, my love [thus Ettwein] - 58

ni eelsija, as I do [Ett: no translation] - 12

ni gechkauwink, my bed [one might expect just "gechkauwi-ja"] - 58

ni k'tahowaalohump, I loved you (sg.) [Ett: "nik'ta-" - one might expect "ki k'ta-"] - 59

ni mâhholohla, I send him [Ett: "nimâh hol-"] - 59

ni matschi, I go home - 59

ni meetschi soognepaassin Jesus moocumink, I am already baptized in the blood of Jesus - 60

ni nachtey, my stomach [Ett: "nin wachtey"] - 59

ni namawemizin, I go to eat [Ett: "nina mawemizig" & 'I must go to eat'] - 59

ni namecamósij, I work [cp. "nemecamosij"] - 59

ni n'daijabton, I talk - 59

ni n'dellan, I say to him - 59

ni nitschan, my child [Ett: "nin ni-"] - 59

ni noch wüwíkin N., my father dwells in N. [conjectural reconstruction - Ett: "ni noch nuwíkin u. N." & 'm. Vater wohut u. N.'] - 59

ni nochquantamen, I lick it - 60

ni nowawaha, I know him - 60

ni nuttammen wingi, I pull it willingly [thus Ettwen - one might expect "nuttennammen"] - 59

ni pentámen, I hear it - 60

ni quáwoohell, I know you (sg.) [one might expect "ki qua-"] - 60

ni quitschemiil, I help you (sg.) [Ett: "nik quitsch-" on 59 - one might expect "ki quitsch-"] - 59/60

ni sognupaassia Jesus moocum, I am baptized with the blood of Jesus - 60

ni wingi endeneep, I was so willingly [Ett: 'I did it willingly'] - 60

niank lalpak n'de, O, how my heart cries! - 58

nihann, I have [thus Ettwein] - 58

nihilla, I kill him - 59

nihillalit, he owns me [Ett: 'I belong to him'] - 59

nihiliwi ika aal, Go there yourself [Ett: 'gehe du selber'] - 59

nik atta néwiiquiik, they do not see me [Ett: 'those do not see'] - 56

nik ochquewak luéwak, those women say - 59

nilannu, my tongue - 59

niiläwoll, my Indian corn [thus Ettwein - one might expect "niilawussall"] - 59

nilhuy, navel - 59

niluuna, we (ex.); us (ex.) - 56

niluna eelsijenk, as we (ex.) do [Ett: no translation] - 12

niluna mpendawatimennah, we (ex.) understand each other - 59

niluna n'dallemussihemmena, we (ex.) go away - 51

nimachtak, my brothers - 59

nimat, my brother [also see "ehohlak" & "kigischquike" & "limattupe"] - 11/38/59

nimattak, my brothers [see "elitsch"] - 12

nin pijtall, my teeth ["ni n'pijtall" pronounced as recorded] - 60

niin tamemensemak, my children [i.e., "nii n'tamemensemak" pronounced as shown] - 3

nin wiquam, my house ["ni n'wiquam" pronounced as recorded - one might expect "wikia" instead] - 60

nipawihump, I stood - 60

nipenáhjak, Summer pelts - 60

nipoop, I stood - 60

nipu, he stands - 56

nipung, Summer [see "ekitsch"] - 11

nischa gischuuchochki, two months - 16

nischen, twice - 60

niskesch, unclean [see "kiluna"] - 24

niskochquéu, a nasty woman - 60

niskpah wemanij, I am going to be wet, through and through - 60

niisquan, my elbow - 60

nita, can; I can [see "atta"] - 6/6

nituneij, my beard - 60

n'kattammuwij [see "n'gattammuwij"]

n'kattatamen [see "n'gattatamen"]

n'kátuk, my knee-caps [cp. "n'gutko"] - 60

n'khahoes, my mother - 60

n'matschi, I go home [Ett: 'I go'] - 60

nooch, my father - 60

nochenna, our (ex.) father [see "majauchso"] - 41
nochquantamen, I lick it [see "ni"] - 60
nojakasgilawo, I am nauseous [Ett: 'it is my malady'] - 61
nolamalessi, I am well [Ett: "-malessu"] - 61
nolamallessiwi, I am not well [see "atta"] - 6
nolanggooma, I bless him [lit., 'I am friendly to him'] - 61
nolapematsch, I will use it well [see "huscatek"] - 18
nolelendamen, I am glad about it [Ett: "nowule-" & 'ich will mich frauen'] - 62
nolelentam, I am glad - 61
nolelentamoohump, I was glad - 61
nolelentammotsch, I will be glad - 61
nolhand, a lazy person - 61
nolhattu, I have it [also see "pischik"] - 61/67

nolhatuwi, I do not have it [see "atta"] - 6
nolichton, I make it [see "pecho"] - 66
nooliechsiin, Do I speak well? [Ett: "nooligsiin"] - 61
noliwunéwo, I do not see him good [see "husca"] - 18
noolsettammen, I believe it - 61
noolsettammeneen, we (ex.) believe it - 61
nonakan; nunaakan, a woman's breast; a mother's breast - 61/64
nonoossô, it (anim.) sucks [i.e., 'it sucks the teat'] - 61
nostawoake allowiwi, when I understand him better - 61
notalauwi, I begin to hunt [see "metschi"] - 45
notschi, beginning - 61
nootschque machquiin, it is, in itself, so swollen, spontaneously - 54
nowaháwi, I don't know him [see "atta"] - 7
nowahawiwok, I don't know them (anim.) [see "atta"] - 7
nowannessijn, I forgot it - 61
nowannessowoagan, my forgetfulness [Ett: 'the ...'] - 61
nowawaha, I know him [see "ni"] - 60
nowawaha nan, I know that one (anim.) [Ett: 'I know him'] - 60
nowawahowi, I don't well know him [see "atta" — Ett: "nowawahow"] - 7
nowawáhuk, he knows me - 60
nowawatoowon; nowawatuwon, I don't well know it [see "atta"] - 7/7
nowewiton, I know it [see "atta" - cp. "n'wewiton"] - 7

nowewitooneen, we (ex.) know it - 61

nowïjoosum, my meat - 65

nowiki Frh., I dwell in Frh. [very uncertain - (?)"Friedenshuetten" - Ett: "nowiki ?" & 'wohnst du in frh'] - 61

nowingi, I willingly; we (ex.) willingly [see "kehella"] - 22

nowingi mecamoosy, I work willingly - 61

nowingi pendamen m'Patamawas, I willingly hear about my God [Ett: '... Savior' — one might expect "m'Patamawasink untschi"] - 61

nowitschéjuk, he goes with me [see "N."] - 49

nowitschéwo, I go with him [see "auweentsch"] - 8

nowoajauwajem, my king [Ett: "nowao-"] - 61

nowoawaton, I know it - 61

nowowilawéha, I comfort him - 61

n'pababij, I play - 62

n'pah, I come [see "elemegisquik"] - 12

n'pakgamma, I hit him - 62

n'pakkito, I throw it away [Ett: 'I throw'] - 65

n'pallho, I miss [i.e., 'I miss my mark'] - 62

n'palsi, I am sick [Ett: "n'palsu"] - 62

n'petauchsin, I yet live [Ett: 'das ich noch lebe'] - 62

n'pijtall, my teeth [see "nin"] - 60

n'potquitehemmen, I chisel it [conjectural - Ett: no translation] - 62

n'quiisall, my sons [obv.] - 69

n'quiisenanak, our (ex.) sons - 69

n'quises, my son - 62

n'sakquelentam, I am confused - 62

n'schaússi huska, I am very weak - 62

n'schingachpin, I am not here willingly - 62

n'schipoomal, my hip-joint - 62

n'schiis, my uncle [Ett: 'my cousin, uncle'] - 62

n'schiwachpi, I am tired of sitting - 62

n'schiwikapawi, I am tired of standing - 62

n'siskelenschke, I dry my hand - 62

n'sisuc, I spit - 62 {as per JR} [Ettwein's Delaware is very difficult to read, here.] - 62

n'sijtall, my feet - 62

n'sukkéhaak kecüak, black wampum beads - 62

n'suppinquool, my tears [see "apampewiwall"] - 4

n'tachquache mauallawi, I will go hunting for the Autumn - 63

n'tallikki, lend me [dubious - see "dellagammal"] - 11

n'tamemens, my child - 3

n'tamemensemak, my children [see "niin"] - 3

n'tappineen, we stay - 63

n'tappitáku, he abides in me [Ett: 'I remain' - "-u" = voiceless "-w"] - 63

n'tátoon, I learn it [see "weemi"] - 79

n'teguiche, I hide myself - 63

n'tehennanink, in our (ex.) hearts - 63

n'tellemángan, my upper arm [Ett: 'arm above the elbow'] - 63

n'telli, I am thus - 74

n'tendeuchhe, I will make a fire [Ett: "-uchwe"] - 63

n'tentalineentsch Lennappewinenk, I will live among the Indians [thus Ettwein] - 38

n'titechta, then - 60

n'tschannestamoosa, I have heard wrongly [Ett: 'he is confused'] - 63

n'tschanilissi, I do wrong [Ett: 'I am wrong'] - 63

n'tschansettamungsa, I have misunderstood it [Ett: 'misunderstanding'] - 63

n'tschinggalen, I have a horror of him - 63

n'tschipalmau, I disgust him [Ett: 'it has a horror of me'] - 63

n'tschittannena, I hold him fast - 63

n'tschittannenuk, he holds me fast - 63

n'tschitschang(ch), my soul; my spirit - 63

nuch, unmarried [conjectural - see "ochqueu"] - 24

nulamallessi, I am well - 63

nummennantschiwan, my left hand - 63

nunaakan [see "nonakan"]

nundéhella; nundéhela, I have need; I need something - 51/63

nundschetochchajak, doeskin (pl.) - 64

nuntschetto, a doe - 64

nuntschimuk, he calls me [Ett: "wuntsh-"] - 84

nuschémo, my powderhorn [Ett: 'powder horn'] - 64

nutalóge, I begin to work [see "metschi"] - 45

nuttammen, I pull it [see "ni"] - 59

nutenakuak, they have begun [see "metschi"] - 45

nutikeuch, he keeps watch [see "auween"] - 8

nutschi, begin [see "metschi" & "metschi"] - 45/45

nutschihillana, I have a cramp [Ett: 'cramp'] - 64
nutschquehan, to be innocent - 64
nuwendamen, I translate it [Ett: 'ich ubersetze es'] - 64
nuwentschi, therefore - 64
n'wewiton, I know it [cp. "nowewiton"] - 61
nuwiquihilla, I am tired [Ett: "-hilleu"] - 64
nuwischassi, I am afraid [Ett: 'I am in danger'] - 64
nuwischassihump, I was afraid [Ett: 'I was in danger'] - 64
nuwullichsiin, I speak well [dubious - cp. "nooliechsiin"] - 64
nuwunakan, woman's breast [dubious - cp. "nonakan"] - 64
n'wiquam, my house [see "nin"] - 60
n'wischási, I am afraid [Ett: "-asu"] — 62

-O-

oochewoawall, their father - 60
ochgitsite, on the foot - 65
ochgoosonnall; **ochgosonall**, wampum belts - 3/65
ochkitáke, on top of the house - 65
óchpenak, potatoes - 65
ochpóchquanal, sides of the body - 65
ochqueu nuch, an unmarried sister [thus Ettwein] - 24
ochquewak, women [see "nik"] - 59
ochquewoll, a woman (obv.) [see "natta"] - 49
ochquézitsch, a girl - 65
ochquí, resinous pine wood - 65
ochwall, his father - 60
ochwee, walk [see "n'gatta"] - 57
oogachsa, the bush burns [Ett: 'das busch brent'] - 65
oojos; **ojoos**, meat [see "atta" & "pischik" & "schewewak"] - 6/67/70
ojoos ikahatteü, Is there meat there? [Ett: 'Do you have meat?'] - 65
olanggomawall, he blesses them [(?) 'he is friendly to them' - Ett: 'segnete sie'] - 65
olantuwoagan, his peace [Ett: 'peace'] - 65
olhattuwi, he doesn't have it [see "necama"] - 53
ooschuwil(ch), swim [see "kneta"] - 29
oukit, a little worm - 65
oowijoosum, his meat — 65

-P-

pababi, play [see "kattschi"] - 20

pachgihilleuch, he parts company [Ett: 'von einander gehen'] - 65

pachhak(ch), a board [cp. "packchäk" & "bakhakku"] - 65

paachhakque, midday [see "metschi"] - 45

pachhakquéu, midday - 65

pachhaquácan, a sawmill - 65

pachhellamen, to split it - 65

pachhiélleu, it is split - 65

pachkgappehumessijton, let blood [see "kneta"] - 29

pachkihelleu; pachkihilleuch, it is torn; it is broken - 65/65

pachkíto, Throw it away. (you/sg.) - 65

pachkschawe, butcher - 65

pachpachk, a ruffed grouse [Ett: 'pheasant' - cp. "poahakcu"] - 65

pachpénnemen, to inflate it - 65

pachtitte, if they come - 46

packchäk, a board [cp. "bakhakku" & "pachhak"] - 9

pahallamen, split it [see "nemetschi"] - 55

paja, I come [see "wentschi"] - 79

pajachkhican, a gun [see "tupálhe"] - 76

pajanne, if you (sg.) come - 46

pajankque, if we (incl.) come - 46

pajeeque, if you (pl.) come - 46

paju, late [conjectural - see "quatsch"] - 69

pakgamaawoll, he hits him - 62

pakgamawoowoll, they hit him - 62

paal, Come. (you/sg.) [see "nakkewiti"] - 48

pallawewoagan, deviation - 65

pallestamowi, do not disbelieve [see "kattschi"] - 20

pallhoowall, he misses him [i.e., 'misses his target'] - 65

paalsitschik, they who are sick [Ett: "paalsu-" & 'the sick'] - 46

paalsoak, they are sick - 46

palsu, he is sick - 46

paluppawachajak, buckskin (pl.) - 65

palliku, he suffers an injury [see "N.N."] - 62

palilessowoacanall, transgressions [see "schi"] - 87

páme., Come. (you/sg.) [fut.imp. - see "ktellauchsa" & "ktell-gemsa"] - 35/35

paame wikia, Come to my house. [fut.imp. - lit., 'Come where I dwell, at some particular time in the future.'] - 65

papachgantowak, they beat themselves - 65

papachtamo, Adore him. [Ett: no translation] - 46

papikanneluk, play [very uncertain - Ett: '(?)Spiel'] - 65

pâpohammen, he knocks on it [see "auween"] - 8

pasitechhi, stumble - 66

paat, he comes [see "atta"] - 7/7

patamaweuch, he prays [see "necama"] - 53

patatamoewoagan, merit - 65

patitte, if he comes - 46

paug, he comes [dubious - see "necama"] - 53

pauwallessu, he is rich - 66

pauwîhellewoll, they (inan.) fall [see "metschi"] - 45

paw, he comes [thus Ettwein - one would expect "peuch"] - 45

pawiuch, she is pregnant [also see "knachchauuschum"] - 29/66

pechó lennito, quickly - 66

pecho nolichton, I will make it, soon - 66

pecho wingtéü, it soon boils [Ett: 'bald ?'] - 66

pechpetukquekhikenk, a pair of compasses - 66

pechchutsch, it will be soon - 66

pehiil, Wait for me. (you/sg.) [Ett: 'Have patience with me.'] - 65

pehíneen, Wait for us. (you/sg.) [Ett: 'Have patience with us.'] - 65

peki, sometimes [see "mingachsa"] - 47

peekok, it has holes [see "eli"] - 12

peeku, I will dress myself [Ett: 'ich will mich an ziehen'] - 66

pelihuweke, harm - 66

peliweke, harm - 66

peemhakkamikeek, the world - 66

peemssijt, he walks - 66

pemmy, until the present [see "allemusso"] - 2

pennamook, Look at it. (you/pl.) - 66

pennamuwon, I do not look at it [see "atta"] - 5

pennauweh, Look at him. (you/sg.) - 83

pennawo, see him [see "gatta"] - 13

pendamen; pentámen, hear it [see "ni" & "nowingi"] - 60/ 61

pendamennéwo, they hear it [Ett: "penta-" & 'I hear'] - 66

pendamenke, if we (ex.) hear it [see "kecu"] - 31

pendilehillak, it moves in [conjectural - see "eli"] - 12

pennundelelell, I will let you (sg.) know it [thus Ettwein - dubious] - 66

pennundellil, Let me see it (you/sg.) - 66

pennundellugun, he let me know it [Ett: 'hat miches wisse lassen'] - 66

pentámen [see "pendámen"]

penthicana, ramrod [(?) penthican - see "mallenítu"] - 42

pennuhl, I look at (you/sg.) [see "schuk"] - 71

pepenáus, a mirror - 66

peschume hassis, Bring a horse. (you/sg.) [fut.imp.] - 66

petanne kechiti, Let me have a little. (you/sg.) [i.e., 'Bring me a little. (you/sg.)'] - 66

petapan, the daylight comes - 66

pétenunk w'tehall, his heart is well-disposed - 66

pethakwonn, there is a thunderstorm - 66

petschehelleep, it came hither [see "phieteet"] - 67

petschichlaawe, Send it here. (you/sg.) [conjectural - Ett: 'musst es schicken'] - 67

petschitawihimook, Send it to me. (you/pl.) [conjectural - Ett: 'habens geschickt'] - 67

petschowalleuch N.! N. brings something (anim.)! [thus Ettwein] - 67

peuch, he comes - 46

peuchil nakewi, Wait a little. (you/sg.) - 65

pewak; pewoak; pewok, they come [Ett: "pawak" on 12; "pawoak" on 66 - also see "elitsch" & "tschinggetsch"] - 12/46/66/75

phakkonum, pitch dark - 65

phieteet, perhaps - 67

phieteet kwikameln, perhaps I will visit you (sg.) - 67

phieteet petschehelleep, perhaps it came hither (the canoe) [Ett: 'perhaps it came (the canoe)'] - 67

pijsqutu, he farts [see "aween"] - 9

piletschitts, a boy - 67

piletschittsak, boys - 67

pili, another [see "woak"] - 81

pilináquat, it looks otherwise [one might expect "pililina-quat"] - 67

pilkisch, a peach - 67

piminatan, thread - 67

pindaquat, it is heard [Ett: 'das gehor'] - 67

pinsewácanni, pasty [very uncertain rendering - [Ett: 'Paste-?-k'] - 67

pischik, indeed [Ett: '?'] - 67

pischik nolhattu oojos, indeed, I have meat - 67

piskau, it is dark - 67

pitschtá eli siikung, perhaps in the Spring - 67

pmihilla, he flies [see "aweeni"] - 8

poahakcu, a pheasant [dubious — cp., "pachpachk"] - 67

poam, thigh; big part of the leg [Ett: 'dicke bein, thigh' / 'die Schenckel, dicke bein'] - 62/67

pochpikaagot, it is breakable - 67

poochpiteheuch, he is quarrelsome [Ett: 'a quarrelsome man'] - 67

pólgool, he runs away - 68

poolguk ahtóh, the deer runs away - 68

pommauchsitam, Let us live. [see "n'de"] - 53

pommauchsowoagan, life - 67

pommauchsu, he lives [see "kella" & "lappi" & "n'de"] - 22/37/53

pommausohaluwe, make alive - 67

pommi, fat; bacon - 67

pómmii, till now [see "neeli"] - 54

ponihan, Do not let me go. (you/sg.) [see "katschi"] - 21

pótataasu, it is blown (the fire) - 68

potawoagan, bellows - 68

pótscheeku, a corner in the house [lit., 'that which is an inside angle' - "-u" = voiceless "w"] - 68

psakkulentschi, a squirrel - 68

psatuwon, German tinder - 68

pschíki, fine - 68

pschíki ktoon, your (sg.) pretty mouth [Ett: 'schöner mund'] - 68

pschiki lenno, a handsome man - 68

pschíki ochqueu, a pretty woman - 68

pschikinaxu, he looks handsome - 68

psintamon, roasted cornmeal - 68

psintomöacan, roasted cornmeal - 68

ptukquitehi, drive together [i.e., 'round up'] - 68

puhilléu, he draws it out [Ett: 'ausziehn'] - 68

putquahull, I make bullets - 68
putqualuntsche, small shot [e.g., 'birdshot'] — 68

-Q-

quának, therefore - 69
quanakquéu, it is soft [Ett: 'weich'] - 69
quapoan, wheat bread - 69
quatsch atta, Why not? - 69
quatsch eet atta aulsettamuwon, Why aren't you (sg.) obedient? - 69
quatsch k'damiku paju, Why don't you (sg.) come sooner? — thus Ettwein] - 69
quatsch lissian, Why do you (sg.) do that? - 69
quatsch schauwelendammen, Why are you (sg.) confused? - 69
quátschemung, Go out! (to the dog) [lit., just 'outdoors,' but used as an imperative, like this] - 69
quawáha, you (sg.) know him - 69
quawaháwô, you (pl.) know him - 69
quawaháwok, you (sg.) know them - 69
quawahêllohummo, I know you (pl.) - 69
quawahi, you (sg.) know me - 69
quawahuk, he knows you (sg.) [Ett: 'he knows you (pl.)'] - 69
quáwoohell, I know you (sg.) [see "ni"] - 60
quawulatenami, Are you (sg.) amused? - 16
queegüm, his money - 58
queegümall, his monies [see note on "n'geegumall"] - 58
queegummuwa, your (pl.) money - 58
queegummuwoawoll, their monies [see note on "n'geegumall"] - 58
quelükquat, it is a joint - 69
quetajaku, an old sprag tree [Ett: 'sprog'] - 69
quewiháwonnä, Will we (incl.) get to know him? [Ett: '... it?'] - 69
quewiton, you (sg.) know it - 69
quewitunéwoa; quewitonewu, you (pl.) know it well - 69/69
quigajojumall, his parents - 69
quikehawall, he heals him [see "doctel"] - 11
quilaween, nobody - 69

quilustammen, I am not listening to it [i.e., "n'gwilu-" - Ett: 'I have not listened to it long'] - 69

quipuumeln, I will eat with you (sg.) - 69

quisak, your (sg.) sons - 69

quiisall; quisall, his son - 69/69

quischassihump, you (sg.) were afraid [Ett: 'you were in danger'] - 64

quises, your (sg.) son [Ett: 'a son'] - 69

quisewoawall, their sons - 69

quisit, the big toe - 69

quisowoawak, your (pl.) sons - 69

quitachpunggewi, you are not dwelling with someone [see "atta"] - 5

quitahemeluwe, I don't help you (sg.) [see "atta"] - 7

quitschechgoona, he goes with us (incl.) [Ett: "-echoona"] - 69

quitschemiil, I help you (sg.) [see "ni"] - 59/60

quitschewi, you (sg.) go with me [see "ki"] - [Ett: "n'quitsch-" at one place] — 62, 62

quoalcheu, there is smoke [Ett: "quaol-"] - 69

quopanachheenhummo, I wish you (pl.) a good morning [lit., 'you've (pl.) lived to see the dawn' - Ett: "quo-panachheenhummen"] - 70

quwingi witschéwul [see "küwingi witschéwul]

-S-

sabbehelleu, there is lightning - 70

sacquelentam, he is confused - 62

sakham, wear an earring [see "knitawi"] - 29

saakimáü, a chief [Ett: 'a king'] - 70

sakomalsoágan, restlessness - 70

sakomalsu, he is restless - 70

salkelentschéhok, pinch one's fingers [conjectural - Ett: 'Klemm'] - 70

sangohille, a mockingbird - 70

sapan, mush - 70

schachachkapeju, he is an upright man - 70

schachachkatákichen, it is a plumb-bob [Ett: 'ein Senckel'] - 70

schachachkeu, it is straight - 70

schachachki, certainly [see "kehella"] - 22

schachhokquiwan, a coat [Ett: 'coat (white people)'] - 70
schagemewunk, straight ahead - 70
schatewiechen, it is smoky [Ett: 'it looks smoky'] - 70
schatschpichhen, it separates [cp. "tschetschpiichen"] - 70
schauwelendammen, be confused [see "quatsch"] - 69
schaweneung, southward [Ett: 's. wind'] - 70
sche bunito, Look! Let it be! (you/sg.) [Ett: "schebunito" &
       'lass sezen' - cp. "schi"] - 70
schehelachtu, Hang it up. (you/sg.) - 70
scheliessak, cherries [one might expect "tscheliessak"] - 70
schewewak ojoos, salted meat - 70
schewondican, a school bag - 70
schi nan Welannetöwiit (Tagauwantuwit) Getannetowiit
      nan nejundángep (natenengep) palilessowoaca-
      nall eelgigunk hakki, Behold! That is the Lamb of
      God, who bears the sins of the world. [lit., 'Look!
      That (anim.) Good Spirit (or Gentle Spirit) the
      Great Spirit that one who carried them on his back
      (or who took them in his arms) the transgressions
      as wide as the Earth.' — "schi" = "sche"] - 87
schichhican, a broom - [one might expect "tschikhican"] - 70
schingatamaacup, (I) disliked it [conjectural - Ett: 'ich ? nicht
      gern'] - 70
schipenasu, it is stretched out - 71
schiita, else - 71
schitaquo, else - 71
schiwank, salt - 71
schiwélemiil, Pity me. (you/sg.) - 71
schiiwelendamwoagan, grief - 71
schiwoapeu, he is tired of sitting [Ett: 'I am ...'] - 71
schuk, but [cp. "tschuk"] - 71
schuk pinnuhl, I come to see you, only [thus Ettwein] - 71
schunnijk, Barter. (you/pl.) [see "juchta"] - 19
schusgoocan, a scythe - 71
schuwéu, slow - 71
schwannak, a white person - 71
sekake, above - 71
seeki auwohuch, since he is known [conjectural - Ett: 'since
      we know him'] - 71
seeky, so long [see "ta"] - 73
sepingquell, tears [i.e., from weeping] - 71
sesachgoppítte, if he is uneasy [Ett: 'if I ...'] - 70

setpoku; setpuuk(ch), very early; early in the morning [see "allappa" & "woapange"] - 2/82

shakkij, so long; so far [see "ju"] - 19

sikkau, it is black - 71

sikei, salt - 71

siikung, it is Spring [see "pitschtá"] - 67

sipung, in the creek [see "machchaquichen"] - 39

siiscu, spittle ["-u" = voiceless "w"] - 71

sisiliesemiwi, there aren't any cows [see "atta"] - 6

sit, the foot - 71

sitall, feet - 71

skapatton, to make something wet - 71

skassumauwi, to light something [e.g., a tobacco pipe — or, as an imperative: "Light it for me." {as per JR}] - 71

skikílatuch, Pull harder! [conjectural - Ett: 'Zieh besser ha'] - 71

sooculaan, it rains - 71

sogahaleep, it spilled [see "Kischellemelang"] - 26

soognepasuácan, baptism - 71

sognupasewe, not be baptized [see "katta"] - 5

sognupaassia, I am baptized [see "ni"] - 60

sooka, Pour it out. (you/sg.) [see "kaatschi"] - 21

sokennupaalittschik, they who are baptized [see "metschi"] - 45

sokenuppassiquik/ch/, they who are not baptized [see "esco" and "neesco"] - 13/13

sok'nink atta, Don't spill it. [thus Ettwein] - 71

sopsu, he is naked - 71

spiechkeiják; spieggejek, a limb; limbs - 71/79

spiegkeiju, a limb ['arm,' 'leg,' etc. - see "gutte"] - 16

sucwon, it is heavy - 71

suugenupássi, baptized [see "ki" - cp. "soognepaassin"] - 27

sukachsen, iron - 72

suksuk, heavier still - 72

sussukahala, a chain — 71

-T-

ta, indeed [see "atta"] - 7/7/7

ta aam léu, it couldn't be true [Ett: 'it is not true'] - 72

ta eet, Where is ...? [lit., 'Where perhaps (is)...?'] - 73
ta eet N. wikit, Where is N.'s house? - 73
ta gunten loogat, Where do you (sg.) get the flour? [Ett: 'Where do you have the flour here?'] - 73
taa hä kähawees, Where is your (sg.) mother? - 73
taa hä kooch, Where is your (sg.) father? - 73
ta ha wundachen kschachhan, From whence comes the wind? - 73
ta k'bambilum, Where is your (sg.) book? - 73
ta ktä, Where are you (sg.) going? [Ett: "táctä"] - 72
ta ktajenden, What are you (sg.) doing? [Ett: "tácta jenden"] - 72
ta ktendanéwo, Where have you (pl.) put it? [Ett: "tack tendanéwo"] - 72
ta kumen, From whence do you (sg.) come? - 73
ta seeky, so long - 73
taccan, other - 72
taccan gischcu, the other day [Ett: "... gischéu"] - 72
taccan kenduwenn, the other week - 72
tachgokíhke, in the Autumn [lit., 'when it is Autumn'] - 72
tachkókajak, Autumn pelts - 72
tachquahoacan, a flour mill - 72
tachquatton tpoquike, it will freeze tonight - 72
tachquichen, it is narrow - 72
tachquipin, feast [Ett: 'Mahl'] - 72
tachquiwi, together [also see "weemi"] - 72/79
tachtagassapan, mush - 72
tachtamse, sometimes - 72
tacu keku allowiwe, nothing more - 72
Tagauwantuwit, one who is a Gentle Spirit [see "schi"] - 87
tahicana A., it belongs to A. [thus Ettwein - cp. "ktaí'gennenannak"] - 73
takkét, I don't know - 73
tallewussowoagan, power - 73
talli, there; in [see "na" & "n'dehenk"] - 48/52
tangeto, little - 73
tangeto hoos, a little kettle - 73
tangeto lenno, a little man - 73
tankhitaak(uch), Stop. Wait. (you/pl.) - 73
tankhitaasiik(uch), Stop. Wait. (you/pl.) - 73
taat, like - 72

tatta matumme, no wolf - 73

tatta mechheek, not big - 73

taatchen, How many? (of lifeless things) - 21

tatthuppégat, it is shallow water [Ett: 'low'] - 73

tatsch, indeed will [see "atta"] - 7/7/7

tatsch kauwin, Where will you (sg.) sleep? - 73

tatsch k'saaki ju achpin, How long will you (sg.) stay here? - 73

tatsch wundachque n'dahn, Which way shall I go? [Ett: "...-quen dahn"] - 74

tauwet'lawall, they (inan.) open [very uncertain - Ett: ?] - 74

tauwiquacan; tauwiquocan, a key [also see "n'gatta"] - 57/74

tauwunnij, Open up. (you/sg.) - 74

teh, day; days [see "Bethlehem"] - 9

tekausowoagan, patience - 74

tekenna, the woods - 74

tekenink, in the woods - 74

tekkennowiik, it is woods [see "eli"] - 12

tendehossij, make a fire under the kettle [see "k'metsche"] - 28

tendeij, fire - 74

tendeuche, Make a fire. (you/sg.) [see "juch" & "theu" — Ett: "tendeuchwe"] - 19/74

tendeuchhen; tendeücheen, make a fire [see "ki" & "nemetschi"] - 25/55

tendewuíwi, there is no fire [see "atta"] - 7

tepelentammen, (I) cease [i.e., '(I) am satisfied' - see "natschnenen"] - 50

tepelentamoowi, constant; satisfied [Ett: 'bestandig; unauff..?'] - 74

teppelentamowi, he does not have enough [see "esquo"] - 13

tepelook, there are enough of them - 74

teepi; téppi, enough [also see "nanne"] - 49/74

teepi gispe, I've had enough (to eat) - 74

teepi winige, it is ripe enough - 74

tepuuseemo, I've had enough to drink - 74

t'gauwitti, little by little [cp. "t'kawitti"] - 74

thataacan, it is thick [see "wusami"] - 84

théu, it is cold [see "husca" & "kschachhenn"] - 18/32

theu kischku, it is a cold day - 74

theu, tendeuche, It's cold. Make a fire (you/sg.) [Ett: "tendeuchwe"] - 74

theuchtsch, it will be cold - 74

thipícat; thiipigat, it is a cold night [also see "atta"] - 7/74

thukenakhakke, so many days hence [always preceded by a number word — Ett: 'the day after tomorrow'] - 74

thunni, Capture it. [Ett: no translation] - 76

tiláku, it is a cold evening - 74

titechta, because [Ett: 'di weil'] - 74

t'kawitti, little by little [cp. "t'gauwitti"] - 74

tmahican, an axe - 74

tókken, Wake him. - 75

topaluwak, they go to war - 75

topan, hoar-frost - 75

t'pettawe, together [Ett: '(we) together'] - 75

tpisgawihillak, it is fulfilled [see "elkhiqui"] - 13

tpiskauwi wikhen, to make the house straight [Ett: "... wiken"] - 75

tpoku, it is night [see "wullit"] - 84

tpoquike, when it is evening - 72

tpusgooall, Measure it. (you/sg.) - 75

tschachachkennemen, to make it straight [(?) "schach-"] - 75

tschappicht, an herb [thus Ettwein] - 75

tschappik, a root - 75

tschei, lips [thus Ettwein — maybe, a prenoun] - 75

tschemammes, a hare - 75

tschetschpiichen, it separates [Ett: 'from one another' - cp. "schatschpichhen"] - 75

tschiesk'ha, Blot it out. (you/sg.) - 75

tschiikhíkke, sweep; groom - 75

tschikócan; tschicócan, a scraper; a fouling scraper [see "mallenítu" & "n'gatta"] - 42/57

tschiku, a widower - 75

tschikuchque, a widow - 75

tschikuwak, widowers - 75

tschinggalguna, he hates us [Ett: 'our enemy'] - 75

tschingaltowoagan, enmity - 75

tschinggattam, I hate it - 75

tschinge N.N. matscheuch, When did N.N. go home? - 75

tschinggetsch, When will ...? - 75

tschinggetsch k'tallamusca, When will you (sg.) go away?
- 75

tschingetsch k'wíkhe, When will you (sg.) build a house?
- 76

tschinggetsch laapi k'paah, When will you (sg.) come again?
- 75

tschinggetsch laapi pewok, When will they come again? - 75

tschipei; tschipeij, a ghost; a spirit - 76/79

tschitanne, strong - 76

tschitannen bambil, Hold the book. (you/sg.) - 76

tschitanneni, Hold me tightly. (you/sg.) - 76

tschitanneniil, Hold me tightly (you/sg.) [Ett: no translation]
- 76

tschitannenineen, Hold us tightly. (you/sg.) - 76

tschitannenok, Hold on tightly. (you/pl.) - 76

tschitannessohali, Make me strong. (you/sg.) - 76

tschitkussi, Be silent. (you/sg.) - 76

tschitsch gutten luwe, Say it once more. (you/sg.) - 76

tschuk, but [see "kattschi" - cp. "schuk"] - 20

tschuk wullesta, Only believe. (you/sg.) - 76

tschulens, a bird - 76

tschulens woaschhichheij, a bird's nest [Ett: "... -schhuch-
heij"] - 76

tschulensak, birds - 76

tulpe, a big turtle - 76

tupálhe pajachkhican, Rifle the gun barrel. (you/sg.) [Ett: "...
pajachhican" & 'Ziehe mir die Buchse'] - 76

tuppekcu, a spring [i.e., of water — "-u" is voiceless "w"]
- 76

-U-

uchtschét, sinew [Ett: '?'] - 77

ukke epiank, here where we (incl.) are [cp. "ika" - Ett: 'we
are here'] - 77

ukit, a little worm [same as "oukit"] - 77

ukuk, maggots - 77

ulaku, evening - 77

ulentschcan, a finger - 77

ulentschcannall, fingers - 77

ummen, he comes from [see "Bethlehem"] - 9

ummenneep, he came from [see "Bethlehem"] - 9

ummennewoacup, they came from [see "kensch"] - 22
undsowoagan, misfortune [Ett: 'possessed (from fear)'] - 77
unemuwon, he does not see it [Ett: 'nicht zu sehn kriegen']
    - 77
untschi, for; of [see "neek" & "weemi"] - 54/79
untschi k'mócumink, by your (sg.) blood - 77
unzschachleo, the west wind - 77
uuschummo; uschummu, a horn [e.g., 'an antler' / also see
    "atuch"] - 7/77
uschummu attuch, a deer's horn [thus Ettwein — see "atuch
    uuschummo," for better syntax] - 77
uussiikan, it is sunset [see "kischuch"] - 27
usikan kischuch, the Sun has set — 77

-W-

wáchganiim, seed - 78
wachkoteij, a petticoat [Ett: 'In. hosen'] - 78
wachpechqui, a bubble - 78
wachschacheu, it is slippery [Ett: 'slippery ice'] - 78
wachtei; wochteij, the belly [see "alamink"] - 2/82
wachtschu, a mountain - 78
wachtschuhattéu, it is full [Ett: 'I have it full'] - 78
wachtschuwall, mountains - 78
wachtuepi, his body - 48
wachwall, eggs - 78
wahelemat eet ju wuntschi, Is it far from here? - 78
wahellemattoowi, it isn't far [see "atta"] - 7
wâholomat, it is far [see "na"] - 48
waholomi, far [see "n'da"] - 52
waholomi n'dah, I go far - 78
wanatamane, if I faint [Ett: 'in ohnmacht'] - 78
wane, there it is - 78
wannessi, Do not forget it. (you/sg.) [see "katschi"] - 21
waschusmaan, (the pipe) is plugged [thus Ettwein] - 78
wasselechchinke, it glitters - 78
waselennemák, Get light. (you/pl.) [Ett: 'Get light for us.']
    - 78
wasselengquechchi, starlight - 78
waselenican, a light - 78
waszit, the hip [i.e., 'his hip' - Ett: 'd. hufte'] {as per TMT}
    - 78

wawiigan, the back [i.e., of the body] - 78
wawoaton, knows it well [see "w'tenta"] - 82
wawulelendamën, is glad [see "necama"] - 53
wawulelendammook, they are glad - 53
w'dachkucumo, he has worms [i.e., intestinal worms - cp. "ahgoganhillup"] - 78
w'daanall, his daughter - 10
w'daanowoawall; w'daanuwoawoll, their daughter; their daughters - 10/10/10
w'dappin, he stays - 51
w'dappineep, he stayed - 51
w'dappinewo, they stay - 51
w'dappinewoagup, they stayed - 51
w'dellaan, he tells him - 52
w'dellaaneep, he told him - 52
w'dellaanewoagup, they told him - 52
w'delangoomawall, his friend - 52
wdeloendamen, it is called [lit., 'he calls it' - see "kecu"] - 30
w'dólheij, his breast - 78
wechijan, your (sg.) husband [see "ki"] - 27
wecuttewall, a firebrand - 78
welachkennémelangcop, mediator [lit., 'he who interceded for us (incl.)'] - 78
Welannetöwiit, one who is a Good Spirit [see "schi"] - 87
weelaquik, it is evening [see "eli"] - 12
weelhik, that which is good - 78
welitamen, make it good [see "kecu"] - 31
weelmukquenk, one who protects us (ex.) [see "gechhenna"] - 14
welsettang, a believer [lit., 'he who believes'] - 78
weelsettawootschik, they who believe him - 83
Weelsit M'tschitschang(ch), the Holy Spirit - 79
welsiit tschipei, a good spirit - 79
wemanij, through and through [see "niskpah"] - 60
weemi, all [see "Jesus" & "jukke"] - 18
wemi auween, everybody - 79
weemi ékk'hokgeewiit, all people; every nation [Ett: 'alle menschen, volke'] - 79
weemi keku ni n'tátoon, I learn everything [Ett: 'ich hab alles hin eschan'] - 79
weemi k'patten, it is all frozen - 79

weemi tachquiwi, all together (the count) [Ett: 'alle zusammen (die zahlen)'] - 79

weemi untschi spiechkeijak, all of the limbs [Ett: 'alle glieder'] - 79

weemiik, everywhere - 79

wendasu, it is translated [Ett: "nuwendasu" & 'he translates it'] - 64

wentenum, to take it [Ett: 'I take'] - 49

wentschi paja, therefore I come - 79

wentschiim, Call him. - 79

wentschiimgussineen, we are called [Ett: 'he called us'] - 79

weppochk, the bushes [cp., "wípoh"] - 79

weschkingkung, in his face [Ett: 'his face'] - 79

weetekang, in his footsteps - 79

wewitaque, if he knows it - 79

wewitawaane, if I know it - 79

wewiton, he knows something - 79

wewitonéwo, they know it - 79

wewituhtitte, if they know it - 79

wewoapsítschik kecuak, white wampum beads - 79

wewoatamwoagan, knowledge - 79

Wewulatenamoháluwet, the Savior; the Lord - 79

w'hokkey, his body - 80

wiecheno, the cook [signifies a male cook] - 79

wiesaaweek, yellow [Ett: 'green'] - 79

wihittawak, an ear - 80

wihuntuwoagan, offering - 80

wijl, his head; the head [Ett: 's. Kopf, das Haupt'] - 80

wijsewuch, mark - 81

wikhen, to make a house [see "tpiskauwi"] - 75

wikkia; wikia, my house [lit., 'where I dwell' - Ett: 'd. haus' - also see "na" & "paame"] - 48/65/80

wikit, his house [lit., 'where he lives' - see "nene" & "ta"] - 56/73

wikitit, a little house [dubious] - 80

wikiwon, a beak - 80

wikquam; wíquam, house [see "allamikquahemi" & "kischwê"] - 2/27

wiktschikan, a breech screw [also cp., "huiktschi" — part of the gunlock mechanism] - 80

wikwahemink loltik, Come out of the house (the lot of you) [Ett: 'kommt herein'] - 80

wikwon, a stump - 80
wilak, hair - 80
wilakeij, his testicle [Ett: 's. m. gl.'] - 80
wiilanno, his tongue - 80
wiilwoawall, their heads - 80
wimachtall, his brother; his brothers - 59/59
wimachtowoawall, their brothers [Ett: "wimachtowall" once] - 59/59
winenk(ch), district - 80 [probably a suffix]
wínéu, it snows - 80
wingan, it is sweet - 80
wingelendangcup, he enjoyed it [Ett: 'kan uns gut leiden'] - 80
wingi, willingly [also see "ni"] - 60/80
wingimaquat, it is a lovely smell - 80
wingku, it (anim.) is ripe (e.g., the cherry) - 80
wingkuwak, they are ripe [Ett: 'sie sind gar ?'] - 80
wingoiwi, it is not ripe [see "esquo"] - 13
wingtéü; wingtéu, it boils; it is done [i.e., 'done boiling' - also see "pecho"] - 66/80
winige, it is ripe [see "teepi"] - 74
wipelateij, soot - 80
wípoh, a bush [cp., "weppochk"] - 80
wipómel, I eat with (you/sg.) [see "gëmauwi"] - 14
wipoomi, Eat with me. - 80
wíquam [see "wikquam"]
wisachcan, it is bitter - 81
wisachkamallessijanneep, you (sg.) felt bitter pain [see "ki"] - 25
wisachkang, rum - 81
wisachkatten, it is pungent - 81
wischalawo, he is frightened [see "kikibisch"] - 24
wischassoop, he was afraid [Ett: 'he was in danger'] - 64
wischassoopannik, they were afraid [Ett: 'they were in danger'] - 64
wischassowoagan, fear - 81
wischasu, he is afraid - 81
wischixinuwe, grab on [Ett: 'greif an'] - 81
wittahemuk, he helps (me) [see "nëmachche"] - 54
witawémi, Dwell with me. (you/sg.) - 81
witawemineen, Dwell with us. (you/sg.) - 81
wiite, go with [see "atta"] - 6

wiiteuch, he goes with someone - 81

wítewok, they go with someone - 81

witéwoll, he is gone with him - 81

witschem goohum, Help your (sg.) grandmother. - 81

witschemil, Help me. (you/sg.) [also see "juch"] - 19/81

witschemuk, he helps (me) [Ett: 'help (medicine)'] - 81

witschewi, Go with me. (you/sg.) - 81

wiitschéwijl, Go with me. (you/sg.) [see "juch"] - 19

witschewoawall, he goes with them [Ett: "nowitsche-"] - 62

witschéwul, I go with (you/sg.) [see "küwingi"] - 70

witschinke, Help. (you/sg.) [Ett: 'Help me.'] - 81

witschisemoomell, I drink with (you/sg.) [see "gëmauwi"] - 14

witschu, calf of the leg - 81

wiwetachpungen, a marriage - 81

wiwewituuneep, he knew it - 79

wiwunitschawiwij, barren [see "atta"] -7

w'láchkschi, intestine - 81

woa, this (anim.) [also see "knennau" & "natta"] - 29/49/81

woak, and; also [also see "keschingquemsaa" & "kischk-ingquel" & "nawe"] - 23/26/50/81

woak âhpitawíneen, And, dwell with us. (you/sg.) - 81

woak pili keku, and another thing - 81

woakesall, bark (pl.) [i.e., of a tree] - 81

woaktscheu, it is crooked - 82

woalhen, to dig a hole [Ett: 'well'] - 81

woan, this (anim.) - 81

woankondis, Greet me. Kiss me. (to a child) - 81

woapange setpoku, when it is early morning - 82

woapaasiscu, chalk - 82

woapeke, ginseng root - 82

woapeu, it is white - 82

woaphukqueu, he is gray-headed [Ett: 'it is gray'] - 82

woaschhichheij, a nest [see "tschulens"] - 76

woawesachkihan, to expel - 82

wochcan, a bone - 82

wochgitatíne, on top of the mountain - 82

wochkitsche, on top [Ett: ?] - 82

wochteij [see "wachteij"]

wolungwan, a wing - 82

wolungwannal, wings - 82

wonnipuk, a leaf - 82

w'schisall, his uncle - 62

w'schisuwoawall, their uncle; their uncles [also see "neca-mawa"] - 62/62

w'sesquim, chaff - 82

w'sigate, when the Sun sets [Ett: 'the Sun is set'] - 82

w'sigate wulaquíke, when the Sun sets, when it is evening [Ett: 'when the Sun is set'] - 83

w'sihooweetup, he conquered [Ett: 'he captured'] - 82

w'siitak(ch) manitu, he makes a gunstock [Ett: '... ein Schaft der Flinte' - also see "mallenítu"] - 42/42

w'taholawall, he loves them (obv.) [see "Jesus"] - 18

w'takkeu, it is soft - 82

w'takkulentschi, a raccoon - 82

w'tamemensemall, her child - 3

w'tamemensemewoawoll, their children - 3

w'tauweeke, he uses it - 82

w'tehall, his heart [see "pétenunk"] - 66

w'tehenk, in his heart [Ett: 'his heart'] - 82

w'tellanewo, they tell him - 52

w'telli, that he; he thus [also see "atta"] - 7/74

w'tenk, afterwards - 82

w'tenta wawoaton, then he knew it well [Ett: 'versteht'] - 82

w'tschintiin, to sacrifice - 82

wulachanema, extol; praise - 82

wulachenáwall, he sets him free [see "Kischellemelang"] - 25

wulakwet allapawe, yesterday early - 82

wulamallessu, Is he well? [see "Anton"] - 4

wulamallessu N., Is N. well? - 83

wülamoewoagan, righteousness [one might expect 'truth'] - 83

wulámoowe, long ago - 83

wulamuen, tells the truth [see "atta"] - 7

wulándeu, it is warm [i.e., the weather] - 83

wulanggunduwoagan, peace - 83

wulanggunduwoagan achpitagoch, Peace be with you. [-"goch" = -"gook"] - 83

wulantowoagan, grace [also see "milineen"] - 47/83

wulaquike, if it is night; when it is evening [also see "eli"] - 12/83

wulásgat, it is good pasture - 83

wulatenamoak nek auweniik(ch), weelsettawootschik Jesu,
They are happy who believe in Jesus. - 83

wulatenamowoagan, pleasure; happiness [Ett: 'Vergnugen, selig sezen'] - 83

wulelendamen, glad [see "nawe"] - 50

wulelensowoagan, haughtiness; self-pride - 83

wullessu, he is beautiful [see "husca"] - 18

wullesta, Believe it. Believe. (you/sg.) [also see "kattschi"] - 20/76

wulestammen, he believes it - 61

wullestammenenook, we believe it [Ett: 'we can believe'] - 83

wulétoop, it was good - 84

wuli n'dah, I go that way - 83

wuli pennauweh, Look well upon him. (you/sg.) - 83

wulilessiit lenno, an honest, upright man - 83

wulilessowoagan, uprightness - 83

wullistam, he believes [Ett: "-stammu"] - 83

wulistawoate, if he believes him [Ett: 'believer'] - 83

wullit, it is good [also see "husca" & m'tachen"] - 18/46/84

wullit tpoku, it is a good night - 84

wullittawe, it is not good [see "atta"] - 7

wum, he comes from [see "kigischquike"] - 23

wunachgutemeneen, he answers us - 84

wunannitu, fathom [see "keche"] - 21

wunatammen, he fetches it [see "auween" and "aween"] - 8/8

wundach neelak, Move yonder. (you/sg.) [Ett: 'Move there.'] - 84

wunachkumawall, he answers him - 84

wundachha, Come here. (you/sg.) - 84

wundachen, it comes from [see "luwanneung" & "ta"] - 39/73

wundachhellapi, Move here. (you/sg.) - 84

wundachque, that way [see "tatsch"] - 74

wuuneígöt; wunéigkoot, it appears [i.e., "wuuneichgöt" — dubious - Ett: (?)'sie sahen' at 84 & 'they see' at 54] - 54/84

wünewoawall, he sees him - 56

wünewoawoawall ahtohoal, they saw a deer ["ahtohoal" is very hard to read] - 56

wunihillalawall, he owns him [see "auweeni"] - 8

wunihillatammen N., N. owns it [Ett: 'er gehort dem N.']
 - 84

wuntschi, from [see "na" & "wahelemat"] - 48/78

wuntschihelleep, it came from there - 84

wuntschim N., Call to N. (you/sg.) - 84

wusami achwon, too strong (e.g., tobacco) - 84

wusami mennéu, he drank too much [Ett: 'too many drinks']
 - 84

wusami thataacan, it is too thick - 84

Wuskaagentowoagan, the New Covenant - 84

wusken, it is fresh - 84

wuskij, new - 84

wuskijpoquoan, it tastes fresh {as per TMT} - 85

wuskikennak, a young tree - 85

wussijami, Smell. (you/sg.) - 85

wutschwi, full - 85

ENGLISH—DELAWARE

INDEX

(please see entries in the Delaware-English section for full information)

-A-

A.   A.

Abide with you.   achpitagoch

abides in me, he   n'tappitáku

above   sekake

acquainted with him, I am well   n'gikinawo

acquainted with one another, we are well n'gikinawootíhemenna

across   gamink

Adore him.   papachtamo

afraid, he is   wischasu

afraid, he was   wischassoop

afraid, I am   nuwischassi; n'wischási

afraid, I was   nuwischassihump

afraid, they were   wischassoopannik

afraid, you were   quischassihump

afternoon, when it is mid   nawechínke

afterwards   elemoqunaga

afterwards   w'tenk

again   laapi; lapi; lappi

ago, long   wulámoowe

ahead, straight   schagemewunk

alive, make   pommausohaluwe

all   weemi; wemi

all, that is   náttchan

Almighty, the   Kettannittuwid

alone   nechhun

alone? Are you   knechhua

already   meetschi; metschi

already, I   nemetschi

already, you   k'metsche

also   woak

always   abtschi

amused? Are you   gulatenami; quawulatenami

and   woak

anger   manungsuwoagan

angle, that which is an inside   pótscheeku

angry, he is   manungsu

angry, he looks   manunginaaxu

animal hair   machhéken; machhiken

animals   awechimoosak

animals, they are   awejajissook
another   pili
answer him, I   nachgooma
answers, he   nachkumu
answers him, he   wunachkumawall
answers us, he   wunachgutemeneen
ant   elícus
ant-hill   elikigamek; elikigomek
antler   uuschummo; uschummu
Anton   Anton
ants   elicusak
anything, there is not   kecquiwi
apparent, it is   neichkoot
appears, it   wuuneígöt; wunéigkoot
are, as we   eelsijenk
arm, my upper   n'dellamangan; n'tellemángan
around, turn you (turn over a new leaf)   klupijan
as   eli
ashamed, I am   nemechannessi
ashamed of yourself? Aren't you   k'mechannessiwi
as   heli
asked, it is   hä; ha
asked, it is   hanne
asked you, I haven't   n'delluktawon
as, like   elkiqui
assembly   mawewink
assembly, there is an   mawewin
as, so   l'likhikquegen
Astonishing!   awich
as wide as   elkikung
as will   elitsch
atonement   mootsch
at that time   elkhiqui
Autumn, I will spend the   n'tachquache
Autumn, in the   tachgokíhke
Autumn, when it is   tachgokíhke
Autumn pelts   tachkókajak
away, I go   n'dallemussi
away, they fly   aawehellewak
away, we go   n'dallemussihemmena
ax; axe   demahican; tmahican

-B-

baby   amimendit
back-ache, I have a   nawowiganine
back (of the body)   wawiigan
bacon   pommi
bad   machtschi
bad, it is   machtetsu
bag, school   schewondican
bangs, it (reports; cracks; etc.)   kanschuweu
baptism   soognepasuácan
baptized   suugenupássi
baptized, I am   sognupaassia
baptized, not be   sognupasewe
baptized, they who are   sokennupaalittschik
baptized, they who are not   sokenuppassiquik(ch)
bark (of a tree)   woakesall
barrel   hallapangel
barren   wiwunitschawiwij
barren, it is   m'hittschiju
Barter.   schunnijk
basket wood   lkacal
battery on a gunlock   ehamhitehûkuk
beads, black wampum   n'sukkéhaak kecüak
beads, wampum   kecüak; kecuak; kekok; kequoll
beak   wikiwon
beans   mallachcüsitall
beard, my   nituneij
bear skins   amachkoajak
bears, there are many   machquik(ch)
beat themselves, they   papachgantowak
beautiful, he is   wullessu
beaver   amuchk
beavers   amuchkuwak
because   eli
because   titechta
bed   gechkauwink
bed, his   gechkauwit
bee   aamüwe
begin   nutschi
begin, will   ekitsch
begin to, we   n'dallemi

begin to hunt, I   notalauwi
begin to work, I   nutalóge
beginning   notschi
begun, they have   nutenakuak
behind, from   guuchwëüch
Behold!   Schi
Believe.   wullesta
believe him, they who   weelsettawootschik
Believe it.   wullesta
believe it, I   noolsettammen
believe it, we   noolsettammeneen
believe it, we   wullestammenenook
believe it, you   golsettammen
believer   welsettang
believes, he who   welsettang
believes, he   wullistam
believes him, if he   wulistawoate
believes it, he   wulestammen
believe, you   gollséttam
bellied, he is thick-   machascútscheu
bellows   potawoagan
belly   wachtei; wochteij
belongs to it   tahicana
belts, wampum   goossoowall; ochgoosonnall; ochgosonall
Bethlehem   Bethlehem
better, much   allowiwe
better, somewhat   mingachsa
beyond   neelak; nelak
big   machhaket
big   mechheek; mechhek
bind it, I   nálambissi
bird   tschulens
bird, male   lennuwehellêü
birds   tschulensak
bitter, it is   wisachcan
bitter pain, you felt   wisachkamallessijanneep
black, it is   sikkau
bless him, I   nolanggooma
bless us, he will   golangguumgunatsch
blesses them, he   olanggomawall
blood   mohoccu
blood, his   moocum

blood, in your   k'mócumink
blood, let   dangkamukky; pachkgappehumessijton
bloody   mequit
Blot it out.   tschiesk'ha
blown, it is (the fire)   pótataasu
board   bakhakku; pachhak(ch); packchäk
body   hackey
body, his   hokkey; hokkenam; w'hokkey; wachtuepi
body, my   nachtuépi
body, your   kachtuepi
boils, it   wingtéü; wingtéu
bone   wochcan
bone, shin-   higachquan
bone, your shin-   khigachquan
book   bambil
book, your   k'bambilum
born, he was   m'hittapitup
borrow, I cannot   gemmakehawi
bought it? Have you   k'mahallumaken
bought it, I   nemahallemmenneep
bound   kachbeton
bow   hattape
boy   piletschitts
boys   piletschittsak
bread   achpoan
bread, my   n'dapoan
bread, wheat   quapoan
break, he will   bugquihellewatsch
break, it will   gachgihilleuchtsch
break it down   gachgihella; gachkenne
breakable, it is   pochpikaagot
breast, a woman's   nonakan; nunaakan; nuwunakan
breast, his   w'dólheij
breast, my   n'dulhaal
breast, your   kduulhäl
breath   lalíche
breath   lechewan
breech-screw   huiktschi; wiktschikan
bring each other, we   kpeschutineen
bring him home, you   k'matschalla
Bring him to me.   peschume
Bring it to me.   petanne

brings something, he   petschowalleuch
broad   lekhiquâtejeku
broad daylight, there is   lawoapanne
broken   bugqühelleu
broken, it is   pachkihelleu; pachkihilleuch
broken, it will be   kachkihillewatsch
broken, you are   kachkihilla
broom   schichhican
brother, elder   chánsa
brother, his   wimachtall
brother, my   nimat
brother, my older   n'chansa
brother, our   kimachtenna
brother, your   kimat; kimachtowoa
brothers, his   wimachtall
brothers, my   nimachtak; nimattak
brothers, our   kimachtennaanak
brothers, their   wimachtowoawall
brothers, your   kimachtak; kimachtowoawak
brought it, we have   kpeschutineen
brought someone, they   bescheweuwak
bubble   wachpechqui
buckskin   paluppawachajak
build a house, you   k'wíkhe
bullet-mould   allohoacan
bullets, I make   putquahull
burn   lussin
burn yourself, you will   klussi
burns, the bush   oogachsa
burns, when it   lutéke
burns something, he   kschassum
burnt, I am not   lussiwi
bush   wípoh
bush burns, the   oogachsa
bushes, the   weppochk
butcher   pachkschawe
but   schuk; tschuk
buy it   mahallammen; mahallamen
by and by   nagajeeke
by   untschi

-C-

calf (of the leg)   witschu
Call him.   wentschiim; wuntschim
called, we are   wentschiimgussineen
calls it, he   wdeloendamen
calls me a liar, he   n'gakelülük
calls me, he   nuntschimuk
came, I   m'pahump; m'paneep
came from, he   ummenneep
came from, they   ummennewoacup
came from there, it   wuntschihelleep
came hither, it   petschehelleep
camp. Let us   mawikatam
can   nita
can, I   n'hitta; nita; n'hittawi
canoe   amoochchol
Can you?   kneta; knitawi
captives   messenawak
Capture it.   thunni
care. Take   nachhaasi
Care for us.   lechchauwelemineen
care of us. Take   anatschschihineen
carried them in his arms, one who   natenengep
carried them on his back, one who   nejundángep
carries it on his back, he   najuntam
carries me on his back, he   najuumuk
Carry him on your back.   najuum; najum
Carry it along.   lochwatol
Carry it on your back.   najunta
Carry me on your back.   najuumi
carry something on my arm or in my hand, I   n'geelennemen
carry something on my back, I   najuntammen
cease, I   tepelentammen
certainly   schachachki
chaff   w'sesquim
chain   sussukahala
chair, wicker   m'hitquapapun
chalk   woapaasiscu
cheap, it is   apüwaawächtu
cherries   scheliessak
chest, my   n'dulhaal

chest, your kduulhäl
chicken kikįbisch
chief saakimáü
child amemensall; amimens
child, he is a amemensu
child, he is a little amimenstu
child, he was a amemensoop; amimensoop
child, her w'tamemensemall
child, I am a n'damemensi
child, I was a n'damemensihump; n'damemensineep
child, little amimenstu
child, my n'tamemens
child, you are a k'damemensi
child, you were a k'damemensihump
child, your knitschan; k'tamemens
children amemensall
Children! amimenstook
children, my n'tamemensemak
children, our k'tamemensemennaanak
children, (someone's) amimensemall
children, their w'tamemensemewoawoll
children, they are amemensoak
children, they were amemensopannik
children, we are n'damemensíhummena
children, we were n'damemensihummenagup
children, you are k'damemensihimmo
children, your k'tamemensemak; k'tamemensemewoawak
children, you were k'damemensihimmogup
chin, my n'hukqui
chin, your k'hukqui
chisel it, I n'potquitehemmen
chop wood giskaquen
clay pot asiskequahoos
clears up, it (the weather) moschhakquat
Close it. kpahîj
Close the door. kpahîj
close to him, you stay kichk'hikkau
close to you, I live kpechiwigul
cloud achchumhook
cloudy, it is achgumhokgot; achwachkummau
clover, green nenchchanipakkak
coat schachhokquiwan

cock (for a gunlock)   mematschéhella
cock (rooster)   lennuwehellêü
cold, I am   n'dachquatschi
cold, it is   théu
cold, it will be   theuchtsch
cold evening, it is a   tiláku
cold night, it is a   thipícat; thiipigat
color   etspinaquat
comb   kschichhican
Come.   juchta
Come.   paal
Come.   páme; paame
come, I   m'pa; n'pah; paja
come, if I   m'pajaane
come, if they   pachtitte
come, if we   pajankque
come, if you   pajanne; pajeeque
come, they   pewak; pewoak; pewok
come, we   m'pahemmenna
come, you have   k'paamse
come, you   k'pa; k'paah; k'pahemmo; kpahemmoh
come from, you   kumen
Come here.   wundachha
Come in.   matemeeke; mattemeeke
come near, I   m'pechchuwigamen
come to you   gëmauwi
Come out (the lot of you).   ktscholtik; loltik
comes, he   paat; paug; paw; peuch
comes, if he   patitte
comes from, he   ummen; wum
comes from, it   wundachen
comfort him, I   neliuhóggala; neliwelendamohóla; nowowilawéha
comfort you, I will   keliuhoggaleltsch
comforted, I am   neliuhoggaluksi; neliwelendamohalgussij
company, he parts   pachgihilleuch
compasses, a pair of   pechpetukquekhikenk
conceal it, I   n'dachkoolsi
conceal it, they   achkoolsoak
conceal it, we   n'dachkolsihenna
conceal it, you   k'dakgolsihummo
Conceal me.   andahelliil
conceal something   achkoolsi

conceals it, he   achkoolsu
confused   schauwelendammen
confused, he is   sacquelentam
confused, I am   n'sakquelentam
confused, you are   ktschannitussij
congregation   memenachpiitschik
conquered, he   w'sihooweetup
conscience, your   k'tellapewoagan
constant   tepelentamoowi
constantly   n'gommawe
cook (a male cook)   wiecheno
corner (in the house)   pótscheeku
corn, my Indian   niiläwoll
corn, our Indian   kilawossenanall
cornmeal, roasted   psintamon; psintomöacan
corpse   allemiú
Cough once.   chucque
could   a; aam
could, I   n'hitta
covenant   ahkekentowoagan
Covenant, the New   wuskaagentowoagan
cows, there aren't any   sisiliesemiwi
cramp, I have a   nutschihillana
created me, You Who   Kischellemijan
created us, He Who   Kischellemelangcup
creates it, he   kischélëntamen
creates us, He Who   Kischellemelang
Creator, My   Gischellemijan; Kischellemijan
Creator, our   Kischellemelang
creek, in the   sipung
cries, he   laalpak; lalpak
crooked, it is   woaktscheu
crossed, that which is   aschtetehasik
croup? Do you have the   kmakáque
croup   hakquai
cry   lépaacu
cup   ehachtubuwing
cut in two, it is   gischgihilleuch
cutting, wound by   m'dukschummen

-D-

dark, it is   piskau
dark, pitch   phakkonum
daughter, his   w'daanall
daughter, my   n'daan; n'dannes
daughter, our   n'daanennä
daughter, their   w'daanowoawall; w'daanuwoawoll
daughter, your   k'daan; ktannes; k'daanuwôh
daughters, my   n'daanak
daughters, our   n'daanennaanak
daughters, their   w'daanowoawall; w'daanuwoawoll
daughters, your   k'daanak; k'daanuwoawak
David   David
day   gischcu
day, it is   gischquik; gisquik
day, it is a   kischku
day   teh; gischquik
daylight, there is broad   lawoapanne
daylight comes   petapan
days   teh
days after, three   nechogoniechinoop
days hence, so many   thukenakhakke
dead   angeln
deceived? Are you   kakkiwallukke; kakkiwalúke
deceived, he is   ahkiwalaau
deceived me, you   kakkiwallij
deep, it is very   machchaquichen
deep hole, it is a   gunalachkat
deer   aatuch; attuch; ahtóh; ahtohoal
deer, rutting   awimalatook
defecate, I cannot   n'damasktiwij
deny   kpassoweû
desire it, they   gottatammenéwo
desire it, we   gattatamohenna
desire it, you   gattatammen; ketatamen; gattatammenéwo
desire something, I   n'gattatam
desire something, you   gattatam
desire them. Do you   kattatammen
destruction   mammukcowoagan
deviation   pallawewoagan
die, I will   m'piwechineentsch

die, they   anggellook
died, he   anggelloop
died, they   angellooppannik
dies, he   anggel
difficult, it is   achwatt
dig a hole (a well)   woalhen
diligent, you are   k'liichponiwowi
disbelieve, do not   pallestamowi
disgust him, I   n'tschipalmau
dishonor him, I   n'danghillawu
disliked it, I   schingatamaacup
disposed, he is well   pétenunk
district, Negro   neskalenkéwinench
district   winenk(ch)
do, as I   eelsija
do, as they   eelsiechtit
do, as we   eelsijenk
do, as you   elsijan; eelsijeek
do, what we   eelsijank
Do it.   lenni
do it, we   lissinen
do it for him   lennemmawan
Do it for us.   lihineen
do it for you, I   lihellen
do it to you, I   ktellihellen
do so, you   ktendanéwo
do something, you   lissian
doctor   doctel
doe   nuntschetto
does, as he   eelsit
doeskin   nundschetochchajak
dogs in heat   awimalachummook
Don't.   kaatschi; katschi
done, it is   wingtéü; wingtéu
door. Close the   kpahij
door   isquandei
door, on the   kepahonung
dove   amimi; amimiwe
doves   amimiwak
down, I walk   m'paskochwe
downward, from on high   abhittawoapanne
drawing knife   lahlhägóhcan

drawing lines? Are you kschihâkikhamen
draws it out, he puhilléu
dream, you ktellungquam
dress myself, I will peeku
drink menne
Drink. menneel
drink. Give me something to menahee
drink, I must nemmenneu
drink, I've had enough to tepuuseemo
drink, we nemenneen
drink with (you), I witschisemoomell
drinks, he mennéu
drive together (round up) ptukquitehi
drunk too much, you have gusamósommo
dry, it is kachteu; ksínaaquot
dry it, I will n'gaasumen
dry it off with a towel bengwiquammen
dry my hand, I n'siskelenschke
dwelling with someone, you are not quitachpunggewi
dwell, I nowiki
Dwell with me. witawémi
Dwell with us. âhpitawíneen; witawemineen
dye it red machksumen

-E-

early allappa
early, very setpoku; setpuuk(ch)
early in the morning allappa; allapawe; setpoku; setpuuk(ch)
ear, my n'hittawak
earring, wear an sakham
ears, my n'hittawakall
Earth hakki; hakkij
ear wihittawak
east wind kachpateung
easy, it is apuihilleu(ch)
eat, I go to namawemizin
eat, I have had enough to n'giespwe
eat it, I nemitschin
eat with you, I wipómel
Eat with me. wipoomi
eat with you, I will quipuumeln

99

eaten enough? Have you   kteppimizi
eaten it, you have   mitschijeksa
echo, it will   dachpehellatsch
eggs   wachwall
elbow, my   niisquan
elder brother   chánsa
else   schiita; schitaquo
embarrassed, he is   lawellentam
Encase it for me.   haanhugwiitu
encourage him, I   neliuhóggala
enemy, our   nematakkundehemenna
enjoyed it, he   wingelendangcup
Enlighten us.   gischachsommawíneen
enmity   tschingaltowoagan
enough   teepi; téppi
enough? Have you eaten   kteppimizi
enough, he does not have   teppelentamowi
enough of them, there are   tepelook
enough to drink, I've had   tepuuseemo
enough to eat, I have had   n'giespwe
enter, you   k'damiku
establish it, you   ktellichton
esteem it   machelendammen
esteem it, I   nemachchelendammen
eternal   hallamacamik
evening   ulaku
evening, I wish you a good   kolakucheenhummo
evening, it is   weelaquik
evening, it is a cold   tiláku
evening, when it is   tpoquike; wulaquike
ever   haschi
everywhere   weemiik
exalt   machkakenema
expel   woawesachkihan
experience, I have it by   nemamatschilaweemke
extinguish it, I will (a fire)   n'datehammen
extol   wulachanema
eye, my   neschking
eyeballs   bingschiwanak
eyebrow   mamáwad
eyebrow, your   k'mamawoan
eyelid   michapoonen

eyes, my   neschkingquell
eyes, your   kischkingquel
eyesight   nemewoagan

-F-

face? **Have you washed your**   keschingquemsaa
face, in his   weschkingkung
faces   elilawejachsit
faces   elilawejakusit
faint, if I   wanatamane
faithful, he makes you   goolsettamoehalguua
fall, they   pauwîhellewoll
far   waholomi
far, it is   wahelemat; wâholomat
far, it isn't   wahellemattoowi
far, so   shakkij
farts, he   pijsqutu
fast, talk   allachpichsi
father, his   ochwall
father, my   nooch
father, our   goochenook; nochenna
father, their   oochewoawall
father, your   gooch; kooch; guchoowáh
fathom   muschammu
fathom   wunannitu
fathoms? How many   kechangquechtu
fat   pommi
fear   wischassowoagan
fear, misfortune possessed from   undsowoagan
feast   tachquipin
feather   mikon; miccoon
feed someone, I   m'pechammaasin
feeling   amandamwoagan
feet   sitall
feet, at your   ksitink
feet, my   n'sijtall
fence, on the   menachgink
fence, your   gëmennachk
fetch it, I   natamen
fetch it, I will   natemmentsch
fetch it, you   knatamen

fetched it, I   nattemmenneep
fetches it, he   wunatammen
fetches me, he   natténnuk
fight   machtakeen
fight, they   machtakewak
fight each other, we   nematakkundehemenna
find   muchkammen
find him, I   nemachkawo
fine   pschíki
fine, it looks very   manschawinaku
fine rain   aawechelan
finery, your   kulelensowoagan
finger   ulentschcan
finger, index   luhikan
finger, pointer   luhikan
fingers   lenschkanall; ulentschcannall
fingers, pinch one's   salkelentschéhok
finished with it, I am   n'gischalooge
finished writing, I am   kschichhíke
fire   tendeij
fire, I make a   n'denteúuchen
fire, I will make a   n'tendeuchhe
fire. Make a   tendeuche
fire, make a   tendeuchhen; tendeücheen
fire. Put out the   athéij
fire, there is no   tendewuíwi
fire under the kettle, make a   tendehossij
firebrand   wecuttewall
first   neetammi
first, at   n'hittammi
fish   names
fish, rod and line with which to   hamanak
fish leap, the   nannachquoméwak
fish-line   aman
flames, it   kuleu
flash-pan   kandschoctican
flees, he   bolkun; bolluk
flies, he   pmihilla
flies away, one who   elimihillat
flint-stone   mahallas
flourish   welikiihillaaneen
flour   loogat

flour mill tachquahoacan
fly away, they aawehellewak; allemihillewall
food mizowoagan; mizoagan
foolish, they are kpettschéwak
fools, they are kpettschéwak
foot sit
foot, on the ochgitsite
foot-rule lussahican
footsteps, in his weetekang
for aluut; n'dite; untschi
forearm napäkan
forefinger joheka
forehead nachkale
foreign itspiê
forget it. Do not wannessi
forgetfulness, my nowannessowoagan
forgive me, you k'miwoatammawij
Forgive us. miwoatammawíneen
forgives them for us, he k'miwotamaguna; miwottama-
      guna; miwoatamaguna
forgives you, he k'miwotamaguwoa
forgot it, I nowannessijn
fork lelchlawalujek
for that elijan; golike
fouling scraper tschikócan; tschicócan
found it? Have you k'mochkammen
found it, he has muchgaminesa
found it, I nemóchkammen
free, he makes you kiegelachchanuk
free, he sets him wulachenáwall
freeze, it will tachquatton
fresh, it is wusken
fresh, it tastes wuskijpoquoan
fresh meat haskeewak
Frh. Frh.
friend, his w'delangoomawall
friend, my n'delangooma
friend, your k'delangooma
friendly to him, I am nolanggooma
friendly to us, he will be golangguumgunatsch
friendly to them, he is olanggomawall
friendly with him, we are delangomaneen

friends, my   elanggomachquik
frightened, he is   wischalawo
frizzen   ehamhitehûkuk
frizzen spring   hoktschaktschessi
from   wuntschi
frost, hoar-   topan
frozen, it is   k'patten
fruit   klitau
fulfilled, it is   tpisgawihillak
full   wutschwi
full, I am   n'giespwe
full, it is   wachtschuhattéu
funny, it is   awihilew

-G-

gave it to him, he   milan
gentle spirit, one who is a   Tagauwantuwit
get it from, you   gunten
ghost   tschipei; tschipeij
ginseng root   woapeke
gird, I   n'glisiin
girl   ochquézitsch
give it to him? Didn't you   milawat; milawécü
give it to him. Don't   miliégetsch
give it to him, he doesn't   milak(ch)
give it to him, they   milanéwo
give it to him, we   gëmilaneen; milank
give it to him, you   gëmilaan; gëmilanewo
Give it to me.   mili; milli
give it to me, you   gëmiliin; kmilani
give it to them, you   gëmilawoowok
Give it to us.   milíneen
give it to us, they   gëmilgunaanak
give it to us, you   gëmilíneen
give it to you, I   gëmilen; kemilen; gëmilennewo
give it to you, we   gëmiilenneen
gives it to him, he   milan
gives it to him, if he   milate; milaate
gives it to us, he   milkuneen
gives it to you, he   gëmilguun
glad   wulelendamen

glad? Are you gollelendam; kulelendamen
glad, I am nolelentam
glad, I was nolelentamoohump
glad, I will be nolelentammotsch
glad, is wawulelendamën
glad, they are wawulelendammook
glad, you are gollelendamen
glad about it, I am nolelendamen
glitters, it wasselechchinke
Go. aacü
Go. aal
go, I n'da; n'dah; n'dahn
go, we k'dahemenook; n'dahemmenna
go, you kta
go away, I n'dallemussi
go away. Let us allemussitam
go away, they allemussoak
go away, we n'dallemussihemmena
go away, you k'tallamusca; k'tallemussi; k'tallemussihimmo
go for, we k'matschewalehenna
go home matschi
Go home. mátschil
go home, I lematschi; n'matschi
go home. Let us mattschitam
go home, you k'matschi
go hunting mauallawi
go hunting, I n'dallawiin
go through. You must eschoochwê
go to eat, I namawemizin
go to war, I natupäli
go up, I n'daschpochwe
go with wiite
go with him, I nowitschéwo
Go with me. wiitschéwijl
Go with me. witschewi
go with me, you quitschewi
go with someone, they wítewok
go with (you), I witschéwul
go with you, I will kuwitschewulen
God, my m'Patamawos
God, our kPatamawosina
God-fearing, he who is mejawillseet

goes away, he   allemusso
goes away, if he   allumsijte
goes home, he   matscheuch
goes with me, he   nowitschéjuk
goes with someone, he   wiiteuch
goes with them, he   witschewoawall
goes with us, he   quitschechgoona
gone, it is   amehelleu
gone away? Is he   allemussop
gone with him, he is   witéwoll
good   welsiit
good, it is   wullit
good, it is not   wullittawe
good, it was   wulétoop
good, that which is   weelhik
good hunter, he is a   duchwilu
gorge, mountain   hilachten
gotten it, you have   k'mischschamsa
gotten none, I have   nemischawi
grab on   wischixinuwe
grace   wulantowoagan
grade, highest   lawelakkey
grandmother, your   goohum
grass   maskíquoll; michasquel
grave   machtógat; machtschijei
graves   machtschijejall
gray-headed, he is   woaphukqueu
great, it is   machheu; mächhêu
great, that which is   mechheek
Great Spirit, He Who is the   Getannetowiit; Kettannittuwid
greatly   gechhena
greatly me   nëmachche
Greet me.   woankondis
gridiron   ehachpusitung
grief   schiiwelendamwoagan
grieved you, I   kschiwilawelohump
groom   tschiikhíkke
ground   hakki; hakkij
ground, on the   hakkeng; hakko
groundhog   makiktschewa
grouse, ruffed   pachpachk
guilty, he is   latqueháu
gullet, my   gundácan

106

gun   pajachkhican
gun, your   k'payachkhican; kpayachkhikan
gun barrel. Rifle the   tupálhe
gunsight, rear   lenapandicu
gunstock   w'siitak(ch)
gushing forth, I weep   apampewiwall

-H-

hair,   machhéken; machhiken; milaak; wilak
hair, animal   machhéken; machhiken
hair, horse-   hassissischqunneij
hair, plait of   ansipellawon
hammer (for a gunlock)   mematschéhella
hammer-spring   mechámet
hand, I dry my   n'siskelenschke
hand, in my   nachkink
hand, my   nachk
hand, my left   nummennantschiwan
hand, my right   n'dellenahawan
Hand it.   lenni
hand it to him   lennemmawan
hand-mill   hentachquahasik
hands? Have you washed your   kischillemsk'schemsa;
    k'schilemsk'schemsa
hands, my   nachkall; nachkkal
handsome   pschiki
handsome, he looks   pschikinaxu
Hang it up.   kschehélal; schehelachtu
hangs down, his head   henawochquecu; henawoquepu
hangs down, it   k'tschihilleuch
happiness   wulatenamowoagan
happy, they are   wulatenamoak
harder. Pull   skikílatuch
hare   tschemammes
harm   pelihuweke; peliweke
hatchet with handle   demahican
hate him, you   kschinggala
hate it, I   tschinggattam
hate me, you   kschinggali
hate them, you   kschinggaläwok
hate us, you   kschinggalihenna

hate you, I   kschinggalell
hates us, he   kschinggaalguuna; tschinggalguna
hates you, he   kschinggaaluk; ktschinggaluk
haughtiness   machelensowoagan; wulelensowoagan
haughty, he is   machelensu
haughty, if he is   mächelensijte
have? Do you   knitawi
have, I   nihann
have it? Don't you   golhattuwi; golhatuwi
have it, he doesn't   olhattuwi
have it, I   nolhattu
have it. I do not   nolhatuwi
have it by experience, I   nemamatschilaweemke
have it legally, we   n'delliwoaneen
Have you something? (meat or bread, etc.)   goolháttu; golhattu
he   necama
he himself   nawe
head, he hangs down his   nawochquecu; nawoquepu
head, his   wijl
head, the   wijl
heads, their   wiilwoawall
heal him, I   n'gikau
healed? Is he   kikau
heals him, he   quikehawall
heals you, one who   kigeéhellachk; giigeehelachk
health? Are you in good   kollamalessi
hear, if we   gliestamenke
hear it   pendamen; pentámen
hear it, if we   pendamenke
hear it, they   pendamennéwo
heard, it is   pindaquat
heard wrongly, I have   n'tschannestamoosa
heart   dee
heart, his   w'tehall
heart, in his   w'tehenk
heart, in my   n'dehenk
heart, my   n'de
heart, your   k'te; k'tê; k'tee
hearts, in our   n'dehennanink; n'tehennanink
hearts, in your   k'tehuwoawunk
hearts, our   k'tehenna; k'tehennanak; k'tehuwoawoawuna
hearts, your   k'tehowa; k'tehuwawak; k'tehuwoawall

heat, dogs in awimalachummook
heaven awossagame
heavier still suksuk
heavy, it is sucwon
heel nangquan
Help. witschinke
Help her. witschem
Help me. witschemil
help you, I quitschemiil
help you, I don't quitahemeluwe
helps me, he witschemuk; wittahemuk
hemp, Indian hallachpisak
her necama
herb tschappicht
here ju
here ukke
here, be achpin
here. Come wundachha
here, is not achpiwi
here, I will stay n'dappitsch
here, it is not hattewi
here, you are achpijan
here willingly, I am not n'schingachpin
hide myself, I n'teguiche
highest grade lawelakkey
him necama
himself, he nawe
hip waszit
hip, his waszit
hip, my nasitit
hip-joint, my n'schipoomal
hit him, I n'pakgamma
hit him, I did m'pakgammaap
hit him, they pakgamawoowoll
hit him, we m'pakgamaawonna
hit him, you k'pakgamma; k'pakgamaawo
hither, it came petschehelleep
hits him, he pakgamaawoll
hoar-frost topan
hold him fast, I n'tschittannena
hold him upside down, you ktapulchquollana
Hold it. tschitannen

Hold me. klenniil
Hold me tightly. tschitanneni; tschitanneniil
Hold on tightly. tschitannenok
Hold still. clammiche
Hold us. klennamawineen
Hold us tightly. tschitannenineen
hold you, I do not k'lennilúwi
holds me fast, he n'tschittannenuk
hole, dig a (a well) woalhen
hole, pilot eli pendilehillak
holes, it has peekok
Holy Spirit Weelsit M'tschitschang(ch)
home? Do you stay at knuttíke
home, go matschi
home. Go mátschil
home, he goes matscheuch
home, I go lematschi; n'matschi
home? Is he at nachk'tapu
home. Let us go mattschitam
home, you bring him k'matschalla
honest wulilessiit
horn uuschummo; uschummu
horror of him, I have a n'tschinggalen
horse hassis
horse-hair hassissischqunneij
horse's tail hassissischqunneij
hot, I am n'gessij; n'giescheléchi
hot, it is (food) kschittêu
house wikquam; wíquam
house, his (where he dwells) wikit
house, little wikitit
house, make a wikhen
house, my n'wiquam
house, my (where I dwell) wikkia; wikia
house, of the wikwahemink
house, on top of the ochkitáke
house, within the allamikquaheemi
house, you build a k'wíkhe
How? Kecu; keku
How many? keaachoak; keche; taatchen
How many fathoms? kechangquechtu
How many have you killed? kechulamähemmo

How will?   tatsch
humble, we are   gettemakkelensijenk(ch)
humble, you are not   gettemakkelensiwi
hungry, I am   n'gattuupwe
hunt, big   machchilawewoagan
hunt, I begin to   notalauwi
hunter, I am a good   n'duchwilim
hunting, go   mauallawi
hunting, I go   n'dallawiin
husband, your   wechijan
hymn,   eccomi

-I-

I   n'; nii; ni
ice   mahokquame
ice, slippery   wachschacheu
in   talli
in, it moves   pendilehillak
indebted, you are   k'dellatquehuke
indeed   g'hella; këhella; kehella; pischik; ta
indeed will   tatsch
index finger   luhikan
Indian   Lenappe; Lenaape; Lennappe
Indian corn, my   niiläwoll
Indian corn, our   kilawossenanall
Indian hemp   hallachpisak
Indians   Lenapewak
Indians, among the   Lennappewinenk
indifference   ajanketentammowoagan; ksinhattenamoagan
indifferent, he is   ksinhatténamo
indifferent, you are   ksinachpílet
industrious, you are   kigelichpii
industrious man   kigelichpenno
inflate it   pachpénnemen
inherited, we   gattemakejanku
inherit   gathamáwa
injury, he suffers an   palliku
ink [? maybe]   ehellekikehond
innocent   nutschquehan
inside angle, that which is an   pótscheeku
insides   alamink

instantaneously kensch lenny
instantly lenny
interceded for us, he who welachkennémelangcop
intestine w'láchkschi
inward allamungque
inwards alamink
iron sukachsen

-J-

Jesus Jesu
Jesus Jesus
Jesus, my Jesum
John Joh.
joint, it is a quelükquat
judgment gischachgeenintowoagan

-K-

keep kachgélen
keeps watch, he nutikeuch
kettle hoos; hoosch; huus
kettle, make a fire under the tendehossij
key tauwiquacan; tauwiquocan
kill him, I nihilla
killed? How many have you kechulamähemmo
kind, after his guttelliku
king, my nowoajauwajem
king, our ksakímajemmenna
kiss him, I nemuchkawoala
kiss it, I nemochkawoatamen
Kiss me. muchkawi; woankondis
kisses him, he muchkawoaláwall
knee, my n'gutko
kneecaps, my n'kátuk
knees, your guttkúwak
knew it, he wiwewituuneep
knife, drawing lahlhägóhcan
knife, your kpachkschican
knocks on it, he pâpohammen
know, I don't takkét
know him? Do we knennawoawuna

know him? Do you   knennauwoa
know him, I   nennanéwoa; nowawaha
know him, I do not   newewihawi; nowaháwi
know him, I don't well   nowawahowi
know him? Will we get to   quewiháwonnä
know him, you   quawáha; quawaháwô
know it? Do you   knennámen
know it, he let me   pennundellugun
know it, I   nowewiton; nowoawaton; n'wewiton
know it, I don't well   nowawatoowon; nowawatuwon
know it, I will let you   pennundelelell
know it, if I   wewitawaane
know it, if they   wewituhtitte
know it, they   wewitonéwo
know it, we   nowewitooneen
know it, you   kwawaatoon; quewiton
know it rightly, if I   auwottawone
know it well, you   quewitunéwoa; quewitonewu
know me, you   quawahi
know them, I don't   nowahawiwok
know them, you   quawaháwok
know you, I   quáwoohell; quawahêllohummo
knowledge   leppewoacan; wewoatamwoagan
known, he is   auwohuch
known to him, I am also   natachtaala
knows it, if he   wewitaque
knows it well   wawoaton
knows me, he   nowawáhuk
knows something, he   wewiton
knows you, he   quawahuk

-L-

languages   elichsilitschi
large   amenni
late   paju
Lay it.   hattu
lazy person   nolhand
lead (the metal)   dachachson
leaf   wonnipuk
lean, he is   allokuh
leap, the fish   nannachquoméwak

learn, I   n'dandlan
learn, I will   n'hittantelan
learn it, I   n'tátoon
learned, we are becoming   kehakkegiimguneen
leave   makamene
left hand, my   nummennantschiwan
leg, big part of the   poam
leg, my   nehikgaat
leg, your   kikgaat
legally, we have it   n'delliwoaneen
leisure, he is at   ksinachpo
lend him, I   nemattamiha
Lend me.   kigawihi; kikawihi
lend me   n'tallikki
lends you, he   k'higauwihuk
lent me, you   k'delatquehi
lent you, I   k'delatquéhul
let blood   dangkamukky; pachkgappehumessijton
Let it be.   bunito
let me go. Do not   ponihan
let me know it, he   pennundellugun
Let me see it.   pennundellil
let you know it, I will   pennundelelell
liar, he calls me a   n'gakelülük
liar, he is a   achgeluneuch
liar, you are a   kakeluwanne
lick it, I   nochquantamen
lie down, I   n'dellichche
lie down, we   n'dellichihinen
life   pommauchsowoagan
life, poor miserable   k'temagauchsoágan
light (in weight)   langgan
light (candle, torch, etc.)   waselenican
light. Get   waselennemák
Light it for me.   skassumauwi
light something   skassumauwi
lightning, there is   sabbehelleu
light-weight   langgan
like   taat
like as   elkiqui
limb (arm, leg, etc.)   spiegkeiju; spiechkeiják; spieggejek
limbs   spiechkeiják; spieggejek

line, fish   aman
line with which to fish, rod and   hamanak
lines? Are you drawing   kschihâkikhamen
lip, your   kschéton
lips   tschei
listen, if we   gliestamenke
listen to him, you   k'tellsettawan
listen to it, I   n'delsettammën
listen to you, I   glistool
Listen up.   allappi
listening to it, I am   notquilustammen
little   tangeto
little, a   kecheti; kechiti
little by little   t'gauwitti; t'kawitti
little snake   achgooktet
live, I will   n'tentalineentsch
live, I yet   n'petauchsin
live. Let us   pommauchsitam
live close to you, I   kpechiwigul
lives, he   pommauchsu
lives so, he who   elauchsiit
loam   aasisku
lock   mochhican
long, so   seeky; shakkij
long ago   wulámoowe
long you   k'saaki
Look!   sche
Look at him.   pennauweh
Look at it.   pennamook
look at it, I do not   pennamuwon
look at (you), I   pennuhl
look so, not   elinaquatuwi
looks angry, he   manunginaaxu
looks handsome, he   pschikinaxu
looks otherwise, it   pilináquat
looks tearful, he   lëpakguwinaxu
looks very fine, it   manschawinaku
loose   l'chachi
loosen   gachpétoon
Lord, in the   Kischelemelanggunk
Lord, the   Wewulatenamoháluwet
loud, shouts   amanggieshy

115

loudly. Speak   mechhiechsij
love, him whom I   ehohlak; ehoolak; ehoowoalak
love, him whom they   eholaatitschi; eholaatschiik; ehowoalatschik
love, him whom we   ehoowoalenk
love, him whom you   ehowoalan; ehowoaleek
love, one whom I   eholon
love, those whom we   eholanquiik
love, those whom you   eholekquik
love, your   k'tahoaltowoagan
love each other, if you   ahoaltieque
love her, if we   ahoollangque
love him   achwoala
love him, I   n'dahowoala
love him, if they   aholachtite
love him, we   ktahoalenna
love him, when you   ehowoalekque
love me? Do you   ktahowoali
love me, you   k'tahooli
love one another, we will   k'taholtihennetsch
love you? Does he   k'tahowoaluk
love you, I   k'tahoalel; ktahoalell; k'tahoolillel
love you, if I   ahoollanne
loved you, I   k'tahowaalohump
lover, my   eholon
loves, her whom he   eholaatschi
loves him, she who   ehoolaat
loves me, he   daholuk
loves me, if he   ahoolitte
loves them, he   w'taholawall
loves us, he   k'tahoalcuna; k'tahoalguna; k'dahoolgunook;
        k'taholgunok
loves you, he   k'daholuk; k'taholok; k'dahoolguwoa
low   hakking

-M-

made, it is   gischitung
made it well, you have not   kulituwon
maggots   ukuk
make a fire   tendeuchhen; tendeücheen
Make a fire.   tendeuche
make a fire, I   n'denteúuchen

make a fire, I will n'tendeuchhe
make a fire under the kettle tendehossij
make alive pommausohaluwe
make it, not malennituwon
make it, they manittuwak
make it, you k'dellenemen; k'tallitoon
make it good welitamen
make it right kitandschitáwi
make it well, I nolichton
makes it, he mallenítu; maníhtu
makes you free, he kiegelachchanuk
male bird lennuwehellêü
man lenno
man, he is an upright schachachkapeju
man, industrious kigelichpenno
many machcheli; machchelook
many? How keaachoak; keche; taatchen
many fathoms? How kechangquechtu
many have you killed? How kechulamähemmo
mark wijsewuch
marriage wiwetachpungen
me nii; ni; n'
meal lócam; lócat
Measure it. tpusgooall
meat oojos; ojoos
meat, fresh haskeewak
meat, his oowijoosum
meat, my nowïjoosum
meat, salted schewewak
meat, your gowijosum
mediator welachkennémelangcop
medicine bîson
meet, we k'taschewewüchêenna
melts, it lengtêu
memory, my nemamschalkussowoagan
men, unmarried kikapawinug
mend in health, they khikëunge
mend in health, you khíke; kikewa
merit patatamoewoagan
messenger allugákan; allukacan
mid afternoon, when it is nawechínke
midday paachhakque; pachhakquéu

middle   lawié
mid-point   lelawih
mill, flour   tachquahoacan
mill, hand-   hentachquahasik
miracle   mechhek elalogunk
mirror   pepenáus
miserable life, poor   k'temagauchsoágan
misfortune possessed from fear   undsowoagan
miss, I (I miss my mark)   n'pallho
missed him, you (missed shooting him)   kpallho
misses him, he (misses his target)   pallhoowall
misunderstood it, I have   n'tschansettamungsa
mockery, he always torments him with   awischachkallukassa
mockingbird   sangohille
moist, it is   ktakpau
money, his   queegüm
money, my   n'geegum
money, our   gegummenna
money, their   queegummuwa
money, your   kegüm; gegummuwoa
monies, his   queegümall
monies, my   n'geegumall
monies, our   gegummennanall
monies, their   queegummuwoawoll
monies, your   kegümall; gegummuwoawoll
month   kischuch; gischuuchochki; kischuchchochki
months   gischuuchochki
Moon   kischuch
more   allowiwe; allowiwi
more, once   tschitsch
morning, early in the   allapawe; allappa; setpoku; setpuuk(ch)
morning, I wish you a good   quopanachheenhummo
morning, when it is   woapange
mother, his   khahoesall
mother, my   n'khahoes
mother, our   khahoésennook
mother, their   khahoesowoawall
mother, your   kähawees; khahoes; khahoesoowâh
mountain   wachtschu
mountain gorge   hilachten
mountain, on top of the   wochgitatíne
mountains   wachtschuwall

118

mouth, my   n'doon
mouth, your   k'toon
Move here.   wundachhellapi
moves in, it   pendilehillak
much better   allowiwe
mush   sapan; tachtagassapan
must, you   dellagammal
my   nii; ni; nin

-N-

N.   N.
nail, my (fingernail or toenail)   n'higasch
nail on   gentaquahellen
nails, my (fingernails or toenails)   n'higaschak
naked, he is   sopsu
namcd   guttschliwindasu
named, he is   lowonsu
narrow, it is   tachquichen
nasty woman   niskochquéu
Nathaniel   Nathaniel
nation   ékk'hokgeewiit
nauseous, I am   nojakasgilawo
navel   nilhuy
near   kichki
near, I come   m'pechchuwigamen
need, I have   nundéhella; nundéhela
need something, I   nundéhella; nundéhela
Negro   nesgallengü
Negro district   neskalenkéwinench
Negroes   nesgallengüak
Negroes, among the   neskalenkéwinench
nest   woaschhichheij
nettle, stinging   maschanin
new   wuskij
new covenant, the   wuskaagentowoagan
next year   gachtingetsch
night, if it is   wulaquike
night, it is   tpoku
night, it is a cold   thipícat; thiipigat
N.N.   N.N.
nobody   quilaween

north, from the luwanneung
nose, my n'hikkiwon
nose, your k'hikkewonn
not atta; attach; attagoo; ta; tacu; tatta
not yet esco; esquo; esquaata; neesco; nescota
now juke; nanne
Now! juchta
now, here jetta
now, till pómmii

-O-

O how! niank
obedient, not awulsettammuwi
obedient, you are not aulsettamuwon
off, he's bolluk
offering wihuntuwoagan
of untschi
Oh no! heekee
oh that jukkela
old kikkeij
old, is not mihilussiwi
older brother, my n'chansa
older sister, his mesall
once gutten
once more tschitsch
one gutte; n'gutte; majauchso; mauchsu
one, it is only guttúchen
only schuk
open, they are tauwet'lawall
Open up. tauwunnij
other taccan
other side, if they are on the awossijajittite
other side, on the gaamunk
otherwise, it looks pilináquat
out. Go (to the dog — outdoors) quátschemung
over, pull something loghammen
overcast, it is achhuüwoau
overturned, it is gochgahelleuch
owl, little kookhootit
owns him, he wunihillalawall
owns it, he nehillatam

owns it, he   wunihillatammen
owns me, he   nihillalit

-P-

pain, you felt bitter   wisachkamallessijanneep
parable   enenthakewoacan; enenthakkewoagan
parents   kicajuimuwawak
parents, his   quigajojumall
parts company, he   pachgihilleuch
past, in the   mâ
pasture, it is good   wulásgat
pasty   pinsewácanni
path, in this   anink
patience   tekausowoagan
patience with me. Have   pehiil
patience with us. Have   pehíneen
pay   anhauwi
peace   wulanggunduwoagan
peace, his   olantuwoagan
peach   pilkisch
pelt   choeij
pelts, Autumn   tachkókajak
pelts, Summer   nipenáhjak
people   ékk'hokgeewiit
perhaps   eet; phieteet; pitschtá
person   auween
person, white   schwannak
petticoat   wachkoteij
pheasant   poahakcu
physician, your   kigeéhellachk; giigeehelachk
pigeon, passenger   amimi
pile   menneluk
pilot hole   eli pendilehillak
pimply   mamki
pinch one's fingers   salkelentschéhok
pine wood, resinous   ochquí
pipe, tobacco   habwoagan
pipe is plugged, the   waschusmaan
pitch dark   phakkonum
Pity me.   schiwélemiil
Pity us.   k'temakkelemineen

plait of hair   ansipellawon
play   pababi; papikanneluk
play, I   n'pababij
pleasure   wulatenamowoagan
plug   kuppaschkhammen
plugged, the pipe is   waschusmaan
plumb-bob, it is a   schachachkatákichen
pointer finger   luhikan
poison   matapasican
poor, he was   ktemaksoop; k'tomaksoop
poor, I am   n'gettamáksij
poor miserable life   k'temagauchsoágan
possessed from fear, misfortune   undsowoagan
possible, it is   lewonneen
potatoes   óchpenak
pot, clay   asiskequahoos
pouch, your tobacco   kschiwoondican
Pour it out.   sooka
poverty   gettemakhattenamoagan
powderhorn, my   nuschémo
power   tallewussowoagan
praise   machkakenema; wulachanema
praise you, I   kolachgenimel
praise you, we   kolachgenimelenneen
pray you, I   kpatamel
prays, he   patamaweuch
preach, I   m'papemmetonhe; n'dalletonhe
pregnant, she is   pawiuch
present, until the   pemmy
pretty   pschíki
price   lawachtowoagan
pride, self-   wulelensowoagan
prisoner, they take me   n'dahonukguuk
proper   majawi
protector, our   gechhena weelmukquenk
protects us, one who   weelmukquenk
provisions   mizowoagan; mizoagan
Pull harder.   skikílatuch
pull it, I   nuttammen
pull something over   loghammen
pulse, it is the   gogochpopetechen
pumpkins   machgáchqual

pungent, it is wisachkatten
pure, he is kschichsu; kschisu
pure, it is kschichheek
put on, not to achquiwi
Put out the fire. Athéij

-Q-

quarrels, she keloolhtoweuch
quarrelsome, he is poochpiteheuch
question something, I n'dellatschimui
quickly pechó lennito
quill mikon; miccoon

-R-

raccoon w'takkulentschi
ragged, it is metschihilleu
rainbow manakquon
rain, fine aawechelan
rains, it sooculaan
ramrod penthicana
ransom elawachtiik
rash makial
read it, I will n'dakkindamen
ready, he is meetennáxit
ready, I am not nemetenakusiwi
ready, you are not kgischenakusiwi
rear end of the body nassiti
rear gunsight lenapandicu
recognize it, we khikkínammenneen
red, it is machkeu
red, dye it machksumen
redeems us, he kteenhalguna
relate it to you, I n'dellatschimogaak
relate something, I n'dellatschimui
related, those to whom I'm elanggomachquik
relates it to me, he n'dellatschimolchuk
remain, I n'dappin
Remember me. maamschálime
remember one another, when we meschaltienke
remembrance, my nemamschalkussowoagan

resinous pine wood   ochquí
rest   allachchimüin
rest, I   n'dallachímen
restless, he is   sakomalsu
restlessness   sakomalsoágan
rests   allachimen
rich, he is   pauwallessu
Rifle the gun barrel.   tupálhe
right, make it   kitandschitáwi
right, you are   k'majawina
right hand, my   n'dellenahawan
righteousness   wülamoewoagan
ripe, it is   wingku; winige
ripe, it is not   wingoiwi
ripe, they are   wingkuwak
ripe enough, it is   depalingquehellage
rips, it   logkihilleu
roast, they   dappuschuwak
roast something? Do you   ktapúsij
roasted cornmeal   psintamon; psintomöacan
rod and line with which to fish   hamanak
root   tschappik
rose up   amüíp; amuíp
rot, they   allettol
rotten, they are   allellul
ruffed grouse   pachpachk
rule, foot-   lussahican
rum   wisachkang
run away, you   goschimui
runs away, he   pólgool; poolguk
rutting deer   awimalatook

-S-

sacrifice   w'tschintiin
said, he has   elowéza
said it to you, I have   k'tellohump
said to him, you have   ktellauchsa
said to us, you   ktellíneen
salt   schiwank; sikei
salted meat   schewewak
sand   lekau

sated, I am gispe
satisfied tepelentamoowi
satisfied, I am tepelentammen
Savior, the Wewulatenamoháluwet
saw him, I newaahump; newoap
saw him, if he newotte
saw him, they wünewoawoawall
saw him, you knewahump
saw it, I némenneep
sawmill pachhaquácan
say lij
say, they luéwak
say, what you elowiyan
say it luwe
Say it. el
say to him, as we élank
say to you, I lellenéwo
says, he luêuch
scab makij
school bag schewondican
scraper tschikócan; tschicócan
scraper, fouling tschikócan; tschicócan
screw, breech- huiktschi; wiktschikan
scythe kischkschascoagan; schusgoocan
sear matagunihcan
secret kimi
see him pennawo
see him, I will newótsch
see him, we newoawonna
see him, you knewoawoa
see him good, I do not noliwunéwo
see it. Let me pennundellil
see it, he does not unemuwon
see me, they do not néwiiquiik
seed mingku; wáchganiim
seed, it goes to dachquihelleu
seek, to natunammen
seek him, I nattonaawa; natonawo
seek it, we nattonamenneen
seen him? Have you knewauchsa
sees him, he wünewoawall
self-pride, your kulelensowoagan

125

send   máhholohla
Send it here.   petschichlawe
Send it to me.   petschitawihimook
separates, it   schatschpichhen; tschetschpiichen
servant   allokágan
set, he (theSun) has   usikan
sets, when the Sun   w'sigate
shakes, it   nenggihilleu
shallow water, it is   tatthuppégat
sharp, it is   kinneû
she   necama
shin-bone   higachquan
shin-bone, my   n'higachquan
shin-bone, your   khigachquan
shine it, I   n'dellaschumen
shines, it   kischâteek
shirt   hembis
shirt, wash a   kschihemsake
shot, small (birdshot)   putqualuntsche
should   a; aam
shoulder, my   n'dekkeij
shout, you   k'manggiechsij
shouts loud   amanggieshy
Show him.   alluuhumau
Show me.   alluhumauwi
shut things in, where one repeatedly   ehundakbank
sick, he is   palsu
sick, I am   m'paalsi; n'palsi
sick, I was   m'pálsihump
sick, they are   paalsoak
sick, they who are   paalsitschik
sick, we are   m'palsihenna
sick, you are   k'paalsi
sick, you are   k'palsihimmo
side, if they are on the other   awossijajittite
side, on the other   gaamunk
side, on this   julak
side (of the body)   hupuchquenenam
sides (of the body)   ochpóchquanal
silent. Be   tschitkussi
simile   enenthakewoacan; enenthakkewoagan
sin   mattauchsowoagan

since   seeki
sinew   uchtschét
Sing.   assuuwi; nachkohomauwi
Sing a verse.   nachkohomauwi
sing well, you   gulasúwij
sister, his older   mesall
Sit down.   limattupe
Sit still.   klammapi
sitting, he is tired of   schiwoapeu
sitting, I am tired of   n'schiwachpi
sit together, they who repeatedly   memenachpiitschik
sit together, we   menachpijank
six   guttasch
sleep . Go to   kauwiill
sleep, I   n'gauwi
sleep, they   gauwiwak
sleep, we   n'gauwihimmena
sleep, you   gauwi; kauwin; gauwihimmo
sleep with you, I   gauwitool
sleeps, he   gauwin
sleeps, it   gauwin
sleepy, I am   n'gattumquam
slept, I   n'gauwihump; n'gauwineep
slept, we   gauwihummenaagup
slept, you   gauwihump; gauwihummogup
slippery, it is (slippery ice)   wachschacheu
slow   schuwéu
slowly, he speaks   gunapegkichsu
Smell.   wussijami
smell, it is a lovely   wingimaquat
smells, it   millamaquat
smoke? Are you in the   guschschachsi
smoke, there is   quoalcheu
smokes, it   goolche(ch); golche(uch)
smoky, it is   schatewiechen
sneeze, I   n'gusquine
snow   chunn
snows, it   wínéu
soft, it is   quanakquéu; w'takkeu
something   kecu; keku
sometimes   peki; tachtamse
somewhat better   mingachsa

so   ta
So!   Nenn
so, was   endeneep
so, we are   k'tendeneen
so, were   endeneep
so, you are   ktajenden
son, his   quiisall; quisall
son, my   n'quises
son, your   quises
song   eccomi
sons, my   n'quiisall
sons, our   n'quiisenanak
sons, their   quisewoawall
sons, your   quisak; quisowoawak
soon   pecho
soon, it will be   pechchutsch
soot   wipelateij
sore   m'schakaano
sought him, I   natonawohump
soul, my   n'tschitschang(ch)
soul, someone's   m'tschitschangkwall
souls, our   ktschitschangkunanall
sound, it will   dachpehellatsch
southward   schaweneung
speak   liechsin
speak, he does not   illuwewij
speak, how you   eliechsian
speak, I   n'dajabtoon
speak, if I   liechsiáne
speak, the way you   elichsijek
Speak loudly.   mechhiechsij
speak well? Do I   nooliechsiin
speak well, I   nuwullichsiin
speak well, you   kulichsin
speak with (you), I   ajaptonaalill
speaks slowly, he   gunapegkichsu
spill it   sok'nink
spilled, it   sogahaleep
spirit   m'tschitschang(ch); tschipei; tschipeij
Spirit, Holy   Weelsit M'tschitschang(ch)
spirit, my   n'tschitschang(ch)
spirit, one who is a gentle   Tagauwantuwit

spirit, one who is a good Welannetöwiit
spit, I n'sisuc
spittle siiscu
splints lkacal
split, it pachhellamen; pahallamen
split, it is pachhiélleu
spoil it balleton
spoke, how he elaptonnétup
sponge käschikan
spontaneously natschque; nootschque
spoon emhoonis
sprain myself, I n'gulquechchinen
spring, frizzen hoktschaktschessi
spring, hammer- mechámet
Spring, it is siikung
spring (of water) tuppekcu
squirrel psakkulentschi
staircase elagkuschik
Stand up. ammuii
stand up, I n'dammuii
stand up, you kpasukquin
standing, I am tired of n'schiwikapawi
stands, he nipu
starlight wasselengquechchi
stay, I n'dappi; n'dappin
stay, they achpoak; w'dappinewo
stay, we n'dappihemenna; n'tappineen
stay, you k'dappi; k'dappihimmo
stay at home? Do you knuttíke
Stay by us. dachchineen
stay close to him, you kichk'hikkau
stay here, I will n'dappitsch
stayed, he w'dappineep
stayed, I n'dappihump
stayed, they w'dappinewoagup
stayed, we n'dappinenagup
stayed, you k'dappihump; k'dappinewoagup
stays, he w'dappin
steadiness glamhattenamoácan
steals, he kemootkeu
still éjabtschi
still. Hold clammiche

still. Sit klammapi
stings you, he k'tangkamuk
stinks, it matschimaquat
stocking gaakun
stomach, my natey
stood, I nipoop; nipawihump
stood, we knipawihemenaagup
stood, you knipawihump
stood up, he amup
stood up, I ammuijánup
stop kuppaschkhammen
Stop. tankhitaasiikuch
stop working, I n'dequaloge
straight tpiskauwi
straight, it is schachachkeu
straight, make it tschachachkennemen
straight ahead schagemewunk
straps, a few gehetéki
strengthen me, you ktschitanîtawi
stretched out, it is schipenasu
strong tschitanne
strong, it is achwon
strong. Make me tschitannessohali
student, I am a n'dandlan
stumble pasitechhi
stump wikwon
subject allugákan; allukacan
sucks, it (it sucks the teat) nonoossô
suffers an injury, he palliku
Summer nipung
Summer pelts nipenáhjak
Sun kischuch
Sun sets, when the w'sigate
sunset, it is uussiikan
sweat, it cannot ksínaaquot
sweep tschiikhíkke
sweet, it is wingan
swells, it machquing
swift ekkulij
swim ooschuwil(ch)
swims away, he bolkun
swollen, it is machquiin; machquin

130

-T-

tail, horse's   hassissischqunneij
Take care.   nachhaasi
Take care of us.   anatschschihineen
take her, I will   natta
take him, they   nattenawak
take it   wentenum
Take it.   natenummoch
take it? Dare I   n'dammennemen; n'deijennemmen
take it, I   nattennum; n'gennimmen
Take me.   natenniil; nattenik
take me prisoner, they   n'dahonukguuk
talk, I   n'dajabtoon
talk, you   ktayábtoon
talk fast   allachpichsi
tall, it is   gunaksu; gunaquat
tastes fresh, it   wuskijpoquoan
tastes good, it   nawipóquat
teach (you), I   luhumelen
teach you, I will   k'tallûhumullen
teacher   achgekútum; gekegutemekque
teaches us, he   kehakkegiimguneen
tearful, he looks   lëpakguwinaxu
tears, it (i.e., rips)   logkihilleu
tears, my   n'suppinquool
tears from weeping   sepingquell
teeth, my   n'pijtall
Tell him.   lume
tell him, I   n'dellan
tell him, they   w'tellanewo
tell him, we   k'tellaneen
tell him, you   k'tellan; k'tellanéwo
Tell it.   eelch
tell me, you   lij
tells him, he   w'dellaan
tells the truth   wulamuen
tells (you), he   lukuun
tells you, when he   looquejánne
testicle, his   wilakeij
thank you, I   anneschik
thank you, we   genameluhemmenna

thanks you, he   kenámuck
that   âneke; nan; nanne; nane; nen; nene
that, he   w'telli
that instant   kensch
that one   na; nan
that way   wuli; wundachque
their   necamawa
then   n'titechta
then he   w'tenta
there   ika; julak; na; talli; wundach
there, it is   hattéu
there. Stay   achpiil
there it is   wane
therefore   newentschi; nuwentschi; quának; wentschi
these   jul
they   necamawa
thick, it is   thataacan
thick-bellied, he is   machascútscheu
thigh   poam
thing   kecu; keku
things, our   ktai'gennenaanak
think, I   n'delliteha
think about it, as I   elithehattamaane
think about it, as they   elithehattamáchtîtte
think about it, as you   elithehatameque
think about it, does not   litthewi
think about it, if we   lithehatamankque
think about it, they   liteháwak
think of it, I   n'dellitheham
Think of me.   gakkelemíme
think so? Do you   ketelliteha
think so too, I   n'diteek
thinks about it, he who   elithehattank
thinks about it, if he   litehamáte
thirsty, I am   n'gattuussaamô
this   ijoon; ju; jun; nene; woa; woan
this side, on   julak
this so   ju
those   nek; neek; nik
thought, unity of   n'guttitehewoacan
thought about it? Have you   k'dellitehamsa
thread   piminatan

three, they are   nachóak
three days, after   nechogoniechinoop
three p.m., round about   nawehalláte
throat   gundácan
through. You must go   eschoochwê
through and through   wemanij
Throw it away.   pachkíto
throw it away, I   n'pakkito
thumb   gitelentsch
thunderstorm, there is a   pethakwonn
thus   natschnenen
thus, he   w'telli
thus, I am   n'telli
thus, you   k'telli
tightly. Hold me   tschitanneniil
tightly. Hold on   tschitannenok
tightly. Hold us   tschitannenineen
till now   pómmii
time, at that   elkhiqui
time? Haven't you had   k'magenaniwi
time, I don't have   maganapiwij
tin   kijhei; luheluteek kijhei
tinder, German   psatuwon
tired, I am   nuwiquihilla
tired of sitting, he is   schiwoapeu
tired of sitting, I am   n'schiwachpi
tired of standing, I am   n'schiwikapawi
tobacco   kuscháteij
tobacco pipe   habwoagan
tobacco pouch, your   kschiwoondican
today   elemegisquik; kigischquike
toe, big   quisit
together   tachquiwi; t'pettawe
together, they who repeatedly sit   memenachpiitschik
together, we sit   menachpijank
told, you have been   ktellgemsa
told him? Have you   ktellauchsa
told him, he   w'dellaaneep
told him, I   n'dellaaneep
told him, they   w'dellaanewoagup
told him, we   n'dellaanenagup
told him, you   k'dellaaneep; k'dellaanewoagup

133

tongue, his wiilanno
tongue, my nilannu
tongue, your killánnu
too wusami
too, you kepe
too much wusami
too much, you kusámi
took it, you k'nattenummeneep
took our sins unto himself, he meyentammennépanni
top. on wochkitsche
top of the house, on ochkitáke
top of the mountain, on wochgitatíne
torments him with mockery, he always awischachkallukassa
torn, it is pachkihelleu; pachkihilleuch
torn, something lawewoagan
touch it, if I allennamaane
towel, dry it off with a bengwiquammen
transgressions palilessowoacanall
translate it, I nuwendamen
translated, it is wendasu
translated, it is badly machtschiwindasu
trap klachhican
tree m'hittuck
tree, old sprag quetajaku
tree, on a m'hittgunk
tree, young wuskikennak
trifolium with the red flowers macschawik
trim-piece, decorative (for a rifle) hokappehellat
true, it is léu; leuch
true, it is not lewi
truly kitschiwi
trust him, I n'haggelanuima
truth wülamoewoagan
truth, tells the wulamuen
Try it. guttschilachtool
Turn around. kudukkiil
turn around, if we gluppiangque
turn around, you (turn over a new leaf) klupijan
turn around. Let it gluppigetsch
turn yourself around, you gluppihum
turtle, big tulpe
twice nischen

twin   kachpéhsa
twins   kachpéhsak
two   nischa

-U-

ugly, he is   machtissu
unclean   niskesch
uncle, his   w'schisall
uncle, my   n'schiis
uncle, our   k'schísenna
uncle, their   w'schisuwoawall
uncle, your   k'schiis; k'schisuuwa
uncles, our   k'schisenanak
uncles, their   w'schisuwoawall
uncles, your   k'schisuwoawak
under, I am   n'gochgawe
understand each other, we   gennenoostawatimmenna;
     m'pendawatimennah
understand him? Do you   kpendawa
understand him, when I   nostawoake
understand it, I   nenoostammen
understand it, we   nenoostammenneen
understand me? Do you   kpendawi
understand you, I don't   kpendolowi
understood me, you   kpendawihump
uneasy, if he is   sesachgoppítte
unity of thought   n'guttitehewoacan
unmarried   nuch
unmarried men   kikapawinug
unmarried woman   kichkochqueuch
until the present   pemmy
up   hokkung
up, I go   n'daschpochwe
upper arm, my   n'dellamangan
upright   wulilessiit
upright man, he is an   schachachkapeju
uprightness   wulilessowoagan
upside-down, you hold him   ktapulchquollana
Use it.   auweeke
use it well, I will   nolapematsch
useless, he is   machtissu

uses it, he   w'tauweeke
us   n'; niluuna

-V-

vanished, it   hallemiwoaniu
veins, your   k'moocummak
very   husca; huscatek
victuals   mizowoagan; mizoagan
visit them, I   n'giwikkaman
visit you, I will   kwikameln
visits, he   kwiikeu
vomit   mameelandamën
vomit, I   nemamelandameen
vomit, I will   nemamelandamtsch
vomited, he   mamelandammoop
vomited, I   nemamelandammohump

-W-

Wait.   peuchil; tankhitaakuch
wait, I   m'bechowe
wait for him, I   m'pehan
Wait for me.   pehiil
Wait for us.   pehíneen
Wake him.   tókken
walk   ochwee
walk, I   m'pummsi; n'bumsi
walk away. Go   allumsouchchwe
walk down, I   m'paskochwe
walking, we are   kpaamsihemmenna
walks, he   peemssijt
wampum beads   kecüak; kecuak; kekok; kequoll
wampum beads, black   n'sukkéhaak kecüak
wampum belts   goossoowall; ochgoosonnall; ochgosonall
want   katta
want, I   n'gatta
want it, I don't   n'gattammuwij
want it, I   n'gattatamen; n'gattotamen
want something, you   gattatam
want to, you   gatta
war   machtapach

war, I go to   natupäli
war, they go to   topaluwak
warm, he is   kischuésu
warm, It Is   kischwê; kischuweuch
warm, it is (the weather)   wulándeu
Warm yourself.   awossy
warm yourself well, you   kulalawoasi
wash a shirt   kschihemsake
wash it   kschichtoon
wash it, I   n'geschietoon
wash it, they   goschiechtonewa
wash it, we   n'geschiechtoneen
wash it, you   geschiechtoon; geschiechtonewa
wash me, he will   n'geschiechemmoktsch
wash ourselves   kschiechtauwihan
wash out   kschiheesowe
washed me, he   n'geschiechemmokgoop
washed your face? Have you   keschingquemsaa
washed your hands? Have you   kischillemsk'schemsa;
   k'schilemsk'schemsa
washes it, he   goschiechtoon
washes it, he   küschichpatton
watch, he keeps   nutikeuch
water   m'bij
water, it is shallow   tatthuppégat
way   anei; aneij
we   kiluna; n'; niluuna; niluna
weak, I am   n'schaússi
wear an earring   sakham
weather, still stubborn   achgumhokgot
week   kenduwenn
weep   laalpak; lalpak
weep gushing forth, I   apampewiwall
well   juch; jüh; jûh; wuli
well, I am   nolamalessi; nulamallessi
well, I am not   nolamallessiwi
well? Is he   wulamallessu
wet, I am going to be   niskpah
wet, make something   skapatton
whale   m'bijachku
what   kecu; keku
What?   aweeni

wheat bread   quapoan
When?   tschinge
When will?   tschinggetsch
where   enda; ta; taa
where one repeatedly shuts things in   ehundakbank
where we are   epiángque; epiank
Where will?   tatsch
whether it will begin. See   gaachannekeetsch
while   neeli
while, a little   lennito; nagewiti; nakewi
while, in a little   nakkewiti
white, it is   woapeu
white person   schwannak
white, those which are   wewoapsítschik
Who?   auween; auweniik(ch); aween
Who will?   auweentsch
whole, it is   messissu
whom   auweeni
whoring   auwimaalen; malowencu
Why?   quatsch
wicker chair   m'hitquapapun
wide as, as   eelgigunk
widow   tschikuchque
widower   tschiku
widowers   tschikuwak
wife, your   kwiwall
willful, I am   n'dajahoeli
willing, I am   lilligpi
willing to be here? Are you   goingaappin
willingly   wingi
willingly, I   nowingi
willingly, I am not here   n'schingachpin
willingly, us   küwingi
willingly, we   nowingi
willingly, you   küwingi; kowingi
willingness   lhillpennewoagan
wind   kschachhan; kschachhenn
wind, east   kachpateung
wind, west   unzschachleo
wing   wolungwan
wings   wolungwannal
Winter   luwann

Winter, when it is lúhwonge
wish you a good evening, I kolakucheenhummo
wish you a good morning, I quopanachheenhummo
with him, I go nowitschéwo
with me, he goes nowitschéjuk
with me, you go quitschewi
with us, he goes quitschechgoona
with you, I will go kuwitschewulen
within alamink
within the house allamikquaheemi
wolf matumme
woman ochqueu; ochquewoll
woman, nasty niskochquéu
woman, unmarried kichkochqueuch
women ochquewak
wood matachen; m'tächen; m'tachen; mattachónel; mata-
      chonall; m'tachinall
wood, basket lkacal
wood, chop giskaquen
wood, resinous pine ochquí
woods tekenna
woods, in the tekenink
woods, it is tekkennowiik
word abptonewoagan; aptonacan
word, it is a great machchaaptonágat
work? Do you k'mecamósij
work mecamoosy
work, I namecamósij; nemecamosij; netajaluchka
work, I begin to nutalóge
work, if I mikeemossijaane
work, if they mikeemossiechtítte
work, if we mikeemossijankque
work, if you mikeemossijanne; mikeemossijeekque
work, if you will mikemossijannetsch
work for you, I migentamool
work it mekindamen
worked, that which is elalogunk
worked, what is elaloge
working, I am finished n'gischalooge
working, I stop n'dequaloge
works, if he mikeemossítte
works it, he lallogeuch

world   peemhakkamikeek
worm, little   oukit; ukit
worms, he had (intestinal)   ahgoganhillup
worms, he has (intestinal)   w'dachkucumo
worship you, I   gollemikitolen
would   a; aam
would, yes I   n'gattam
wound   m'schakaano
wound by cutting   m'dukschummen
write   lekhike
write, I   n'dellekhíke
write it,   lekhamen
writing, I am finished   kschichhíke
written, it is   lekhásu
wrong, I am   n'tschanilissi
wrong, I do   n'tschanilissi
wrongly, I have heard   n'tschannestamoosa
wrongly, you do it   kpallitoon

-Y-

year, next   gachtingetsch
years old   kachtiname
yellow   wiesaaweek
yes   kella
yesterday   wulakwet
yet, not   esco; esquo; esquaata; neesco; nescota
yet live, I   n'petauchsin
yonder   neelak; nelak; wundach
you   k'; ki; kiluwa
you, I see   newull
you come to   kemauwi
you too   kepe
your   ki
yourself   nihiliwi

Also available in the ALR Supplement Series

A Synopsis of the Indian Tribes within the United States, etc.
by Albert Gallatin (1836)

Sagard's Dictionary of Huron,
by Gabriel Sagard, edited by John Steckley (2009)

Delaware Indian Language of 1824,
by C.C. Trowbridge, edited by James A. Rementer (2011)

For more information on this series, see our website at:
http://www.evolpub.com/ALR/ALRSupplement.html

www.ingramcontent.com/pod-product-compliance
Lightning Source LLC
Chambersburg PA
CBHW020355100426
42812CB00001B/70